HOCKEY

The Skills of the Game

JOHN CADMAN

THE CROWOOD PRESS

First published in 1985 by
The Crowood Press Ltd
Ramsbury, Marlborough
Wiltshire SN8 2HR

© John Cadman 1985

This impression 1995

British Library Cataloguing-in-Publication Data

Cadman, John, 1934-
  Hockey : the skills of the game. — (Crowood sports books)
  1. Field hockey
  I. Title
  796.35'5   GV1017.H7

  ISBN 1 85223 767 8

Acknowledgements

Figs 3, 11, 12, 13, 14, 17 and 32 were supplied by Richard Gardner;
Figs 5, 6, 16, 18, 19, 20, 27, 41 and 44 by Peter Luck; Figs 7, 31, 42
and 108 by Morley Pecker; Figs 21 and 22 by Alan Rushton; other
photographs are by the author.

Line illustrations by Vanetta Joffe and Annette Findlay.

Cover photograph courtesy of Allsport Photographic Ltd

Series Adviser David Bunker, Lecturer, Loughborough University

Typeset by Inforum Ltd, Portsmouth.
Printed and bound in Great Britain by Redwood Books, Trowbridge.

Contents

John Cadman is a highly experienced hockey player and coach. He played county hockey for eleven years and represented England and Great Britain in a total of twenty-seven internationals, including the 1964 Olympic Games. He was appointed National Coach by the Hockey Association in 1970, Chief National Coach in 1975, and Director of Coaching 1980–85. He is also an FIH Coach and has been coach to Cambridge University since 1984.

After eight years in the Sports Surfacing business he has now established his own Sports Surfacing Consultancy.

John Cadman is a highly respected coach who has worked with individuals and teams at all levels in hockey. In this book, which provides an excellent foundation for high quality performance, John calls upon his wide-ranging experience as player, coach and coach educator. The result is a volume full of information that will help enhance individual and team performance.

David Whitaker
Great Britain and England Team Coach

Introduction

International hockey, played on artificial grass, is a fast, exciting game requiring high levels of individual skill, tactical awareness and mental and physical fitness. Many hours of hard work by coaches and players go into preparing teams to meet the demands of modern day tournaments. There may appear to be a gap so large between international hockey and club or school hockey that it is difficult to appreciate the relevance of one to the other. However, the performance of top class players is important to the beginner and what he learns. The international player's method of performing skills is the language of the game, from which coaches have to select the basic grammar to teach beginners to develop into accomplished hockey players.

The problem many coaches have is keeping up with developments in the game; changes in the rules, different surfaces and increasing amounts of competition, all change the language and, therefore, the basic grammar. Too many coaches are teaching youngsters what they were taught many years ago, which may eventually be detrimental to a youngster's progress and cause him or her to have to unlearn techniques before developing the modern methods that allow the individual to cope with the modern game of hockey. The simplest example of this is the basic grip taught to children. The left hand grip on the stick, properly taught, allows the individual to develop a range of stick handling skills easily. If not taught correctly, rnany skills are difficult to master, and the child's progress may be hampered.

SKILLS

Skills form an integral part of the game. Tactical moves succeed or break down as a result of well performed, or poorly performed skills respectively. Coaches must be able to identify errors as they occur in individual, or group play. Having identified the fault coaches must eradicate the error from the player's repertoire making the individual a more effective team player. In some cases this may be a minor adjustment or in some a major change to a player's technique.

To achieve this coaches have to have an understanding of the considerable detail of each technique and how much to alter a player's technique to improve the individual's performance. Practices must be realistic and reflect the aspects of the game in which the weakness was observed. Small team games must reflect game-like activities.

Presentation

How material is presented to young players in skill-learning situations is critical. The coach's ability to demonstrate each technique is extremely important. If a demonstration is good and practices are well structured, the minimum amount of information is required to ensure the practice is successful. The combination of demonstration and practice may have given the youngster adequate knowledge to perform the skill in question. The coach must have a thorough knowledge of all aspects of techniques, skill situations and tactics, so that where a player cannot cope, the coach is able to select the necessary information to enable the individual to overcome the problem. While the extent of the coach's knowledge has to be considerable, the amount of information given to an individual to overcome a particular problem must be the minimum necessary to solve the problem.

Well-structured, progressive practices will enable the learner to progress in a logical way. Some players will progress more quickly than others, and the coach must ensure that groups of players are allowed to progress at optimum speed to realise their full potential.

CLUBS AND SCHOOLS

Recent developments in clubs have seen parallel coaching activities to those in schools. School hockey tends to fall into two sections:

1. Those who play hockey as a traditional inter-school sport, the activity forming part of a broadly based PE programme.
2. Those who include hockey as an activity within the PE programme but not as an inter-school activity.

The weakness of the second is that the individuals who develop an interest for the game are unable to enjoy the excitement of competition. Clubs have become aware of this problem, and that of ensuring that young players, the life blood of any club, have the opportunity to play competitive hockey within the club. Youth sections which include mini-hockey, seven-a-side hockey and colts teams have been formed to give the opportunity for young players to continue their involvement with the game in a new environment. Club activities of this kind should be encouraged and expanded to ensure that those children who wish to experience competitive hockey are given the

opportunity. Clubs must strive to increase their links with schools.

THE BASIC GRAMMAR

The age at which youngsters are introduced to hockey varies from eight to fourteen years, and for some even later. It is therefore very difficult, if not impossible, to say what should be taught at any particular age. A better approach is to consider development in stages.

Stage 1 The beginner.
Stage 2 The developer.
Stage 3 The improving player.
Stage 4 The advanced player.

The period of time an individual remains at each stage will depend on their ability to assimilate knowledge and transfer this into a well-moulded performance based on good habits and on the quality of coaching and guidance the individual receives.

The basic grammar of the game well presented, thoroughly learned and understood will become the base from which high level performance can develop. Only very few individuals are going to become international players, some will not even play for their school, but what is taught initially must enable those who are going to reach high levels to do so without having to unlearn basic skills which have been wrongly taught in the early stages.

Fig 1 shows a gradual development of skill, tactical play, fitness and mental awareness through the various stages. To assess the basic grammar of the game, we have to analyse these four areas and decide what must be taught in the initial stages to allow a player to develop to the highest possible level. Some will not reach beyond Stage 1, but all hopefully will enjoy their game, and their enjoyment will be greater if they have acquired a sound basic grammar.

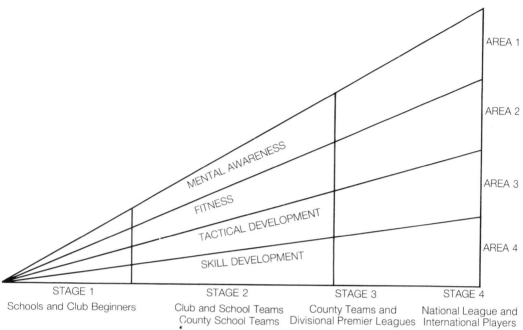

AREA 1

AREA 2

AREA 3

AREA 4

MENTAL AWARENESS

FITNESS

TACTICAL DEVELOPMENT

SKILL DEVELOPMENT

STAGE 1	STAGE 2	STAGE 3	STAGE 4
Schools and Club Beginners	Club and School Teams County School Teams	County Teams and Divisional Premier Leagues	National League and International Players

Fig 1   Stages of development.

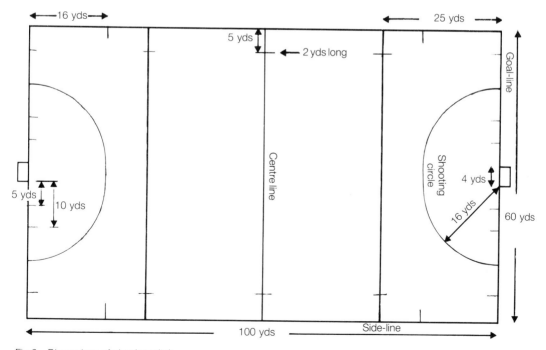

16 yds

25 yds

5 yds

2 yds long

Goal-line

Centre line

Shooting circle

4 yds

5 yds

10 yds

16 yds

60 yds

100 yds

Side-line

Fig 2   Dimensions of a hockey pitch.

THE PRODUCTION OF HOCKEY PLAYERS

Hockey in the 1990s faces a possible developmental problem with a division between those who play on synthetic grass and those who play on natural grass. As the 90s proceed more and more young players will have learnt the game on synthetic grass pitches who may not want to play on natural grass when they leave school. The time will come when every club will require access to synthetic grass for all its teams. The synthetic grass game requires players who have all round ability in terms of skill and tactical awareness. Having acquired these all-round skills, players will specialise in playing in particular positions or areas of the field. Premature involvement in the eleven-a-side game often restricts an individual's development as a hockey player. Small-sided games give greater opportunity to increase contact with the ball and the chance to understand involvement within a team more thoroughly.

Coaches should appreciate the value of mini-hockey and seven-a-side hockey for those in the first stage of their development.

Very young players must also be provided with suitable equipment to make learning easier. Small sticks from 30 to 34 inches are now available, plus special mini-hockey balls. This equipment has revolutionised the introduction of hockey to the eight to ten age group.

To ensure that good all-round hockey players are produced, coaches must carefully examine what they are doing and continually re-assess their work to ensure they are giving their young players the best opportunity to progress.

COMPETITION

There is a danger that, in the early stages of individual development, competition becomes too important a factor in the hockey programme. Competition is an essential element in any hockey programme, but it must be well structured. Competition which is well controlled is healthy but young players require a sound balance of coaching and competition. Mini-Hockey age group players should, for example, be given a balanced menu of three coaching sessions to each competitive game or tournament.

1 Skills

Effective attacking team play depends largely on each individual performing skills well in every tactical move. Each time a player receives a ball, passes it, or moves on their own with the ball a *skill point* is established. The player may be required to receive the ball from the right, control it and push the ball to a player in support on his left. On other occasions it may be necessary to receive the ball from in front of the body, control it, create space and then hit it to a player wide on the left of the field. In each instance the ball will have been received by different methods, controlled, then space created and the ball passed using one of two methods – the push and the hit. To perform skills effectively, players have to learn the basic methods of stick handling, receiving and controlling the ball, and passing.

It is essential that players acquire the ability to handle the stick effectively in differing circumstances, appreciating the variations in hand positions, stick angle and body positions. The variations in the grip will be explained in each skill, but the starting point must be the grip adopted for individual ball control. Players must be able to play the ball equally well on the left of the body (the reverse side) and on the right (the open side).

The starting point must be the basic grammar of skill which can be developed as players progress into the language of hockey, as they express their own individual style in the future. Coaches, as players develop after being introduced to the basic grammar, must judge a player on his effectiveness, not necessarily the aesthetic look of a skill as it is performed. Players develop as individuals and must not be produced as stereotypes. Great players have based their games on good basics but have added their own individual flair and style. The order in which the skills of the game are listed here is an order in which coaches may consider introducing skills to young players.

INDIVIDUAL BALL CONTROL

Grip *(Figs 3 to 5)*

The left hand is placed near the top of the stick with the 'V' formed by the thumb and the first finger down the back of the stick. Holding the stick out in front of the body, in this way, will result in the flat hitting face of the stick facing to the ground. The right hand is placed down the stick.

To move the stick from the reverse stick position to the open stick position turn it with the left hand. The stick turns in the right hand which assists in controlling the position of the stick.

Vision *(Figs 6 & 7)*

When controlling the ball, a player must be able to see as much as possible of what is occurring over the rest of the pitch. The position in which the ball is controlled in relation to the body will assist good vision. If the ball is well away from the body and the upper body inclined forwards, the player will have good vision of what his team-mates and opponents are doing. If the upper body is bent over the ball, because

Fig 3 Note position of left hand at top of stick and angle of stick in front of body.

the ball is being controlled too close to the feet, the individual's vision will be reduced.

To move at speed, it is important to keep the ball in a position which allows the legs room to run in a natural way. Again the ball must be kept well out in front of the body. The ball should be in front of, or just outside, the right foot. If the ball veers to the left, it should be readjusted by turning the stick to the reverse position and moving the ball back to the open side, the strong position.

When opponents are near to the player with the ball, close control is necessary. It is important that in obtaining closer control, vision is not restricted. The centre of gravity must be lowered and shorter, faster strides taken to give greater mobility and maintain tactical awareness.

Fig 4 The correct grip.

Fig 5   Note good ball position allowing good vision.

Fig 6   Note position of ball in relation to body; player able to look up.

Footwork

Balanced footwork is an essential part of a good player's repertoire. The ability to move forwards, backwards and sideways while controlling the ball; changing direction and pace while approaching an opponent must be mastered by all players. The motto *footwork before control* should be ingrained into every player's mind. When this is achieved players put themselves in strong positions before receiving the ball, avoiding getting into trouble because their footwork is inadequate.

Note

If a player has to control the ball on the reverse side of the body he must move it to the open side, *the strong side*, as quickly as possible.

Fig 7   Close control has been achieved
without restricting vision.

PASSING THE BALL

The methods of passing the ball can be categorised as follows:

The push pass – open stick and reverse stick.
The hit.
The flick.
The aerial ball – scoop and flick.

Each of these methods of passing has to be subdivided to cover passing to the left, right and forwards. However, each has a basic movement from which variations of foot position and body position are made.

With all methods of passing, players and coaches should consider the following points:

1. The position of the head.
2. The position of the shoulders.
3. The position of the feet.
4. The position of the hands on the stick.
5. The transfer of weight from the right foot to the left foot.
6. The follow-through of the stick, hands and arms into the stroke.

In some instances all elements will be relevant, in others only some can be covered. For example, when pushing the ball from left to right in open space, the whole body can be brought round to ensure the most effective pushing position.

All the six elements mentioned above must be considered when looking at the methods of passing. In the following text, they will not be mentioned independently except where specific reference is required.

Fig 8   Starting position for a push.

Fig 9   Body weight and stick start to move forward.

Fig 10   Body weight forward, stick
following through.

Push *(Figs 8 to 13)*

The push is the method of passing used to pass the ball mainly over short distances, though good players are able to push the ball over considerable distances on synthetic grass. It is also the method which gives your opponent least indication of where and when you are going to pass.

It will be noticed that the left hand grip on the stick has changed (see *Fig 4*), while the right hand remains down the stick, though not too far down or an effective pushing position is lost. The ball starts between the feet, with the stick in contact with the ball. The left side of the body points in the direction of the push. As the body weight moves forward, the ball is moved forward in the direction of the push. The final movement of the ball brings the stick into the follow-through position. The stick should be kept in contact with the ball as long

as possible, thus adding to the accuracy and power of the push. The follow-through will assist the accuracy of the pass, the lower position of the body will give added power.

The push pass is most often performed on the move, therefore players must practise this way rather than in the static position. Players will also be required to push the ball in varying directions and off either foot. Often there is not time or space to get into the ideal position. The player has to perform the skill in a variety of ways – to the right, to the front, to the left and off the right foot. Practices must reflect this.

Reverse Stick Push
(Figs 14 & 15)

The reverse stick push is played, as suggested, with the stick in the reverse position. It is used to pass the ball from left to right over a

Fig 11   Follow-through position with eyes
          following ball.

Fig 12   Body is lowered to gain more drive
          from right leg, giving extra power.

Fig 13   Body position low, right arm
producing strong movement into
follow-through.

short distance, often to a player moving up in support. It is a pass that can be made without giving any indication to the opponent when, and in what direction, the pass will be made. The pass is made from the opponent's strong position (his open side) across his body to his reverse side (his weaker side). More often than not, a reverse stick pass is one played square or behind square.

Hit *(Figs 16 & 17)*

The hit is used for passes over longer distances than the push can achieve, for shooting at goal, and when taking free-hits or hit-ins.

The grip on the stick changes. The left hand is placed near the top of the stick with the 'V' formed by the first finger and thumb down the edge of the stick. The right hand is brought up the handle to be in contact with the left hand. This is the only time when the hands are together on the stick.

The basic hitting technique has to be seen in three parts:

1. The backlift. The stick is taken back as the left foot moves towards the ball; the wrists are cocked. Note that a high backlift is not necessary and often leads to dangerous play.
2. The hit. The body weight has been transferred to the left foot and the head brought over the ball. The ball is not too near the body, causing a cramped up position, or too far from the body which causes reaching. Both these faults would reduce the effectiveness of the hit.
3. The follow-through. The stick, hands and

Fig 14 Short pass left to right – note left hand position on stick and body position.

Fig 15 Reverse stick push – note toe of stick in reverse position.

arms follow through in the direction of the hit, assisting accuracy and power.

Players have to learn to master hitting a stationary ball as well as a moving ball when they are moving. As with the push adjustments of feet and body positions have to be made to hit to the right, to the left and infront of the body, particularly when shooting at goal.

Flick *(Figs 18 to 20)*

The flick should be seen as an extension to the push, the difference being that the push is played along the ground, whereas the flick is played in the air to move the ball over an opponent's stick or to lift the ball when shooting at goal. A flick is often used for a penalty stroke. The flick is used over longer distances than the push but not over the distances covered by a long hit. The flick, in its basic

Fig 16 *Players must also learn to hit off the right foot.*

Fig 17 *Ball struck, eyes still looking at point of hit.*

form, should not be confused with the aerial pass.

While similar to the push, the starting point of the stroke is with the ball level with the front foot and the stick inclined. The stick is in contact with the ball as in the push and the grip is similar, though the hands may be slightly closer together. The weight of the body starts more on the right foot than in the push.

As the flick is performed, the stick is kept in contact with the ball as long as possible and held as far away from the body as possible. The weight of the body is brought forward and over the left leg as the stick is brought into the follow-through position. Note that to give the final impulse to the ball, the right hand turns the stick to bring the toe of the stick into an upright position.

Players must master flicking the ball to the left and right while on the move. Like the hit and push, the flick is a sideways-on movement.

Aerial Flick

Once the basic flick has been mastered, players should attempt to play the stroke over longer distances, gaining greater heights. Many top class players can now play the aerial ball over 40 to 50 metres. Such a stroke can be used to put the ball in behind opposition defences for forwards to move on to.

The aerial flick can also be used for playing the ball over opponents to a player only 10 – 15 metres away, lifting the ball over the opponent into space behind him. Both the long and short pass should be acquired by players. Technique is important but strength in the forearm, particularly the right forearm, is a great advantage.

Scoop

A less effective aerial pass is the scoop. The

15

Fig 18   Flick – starting position further
          forward than for the push.

Fig 19   The ball is flicked into the air.

Fig 20   Follow-through well away from the
          body; the ball is kept in contact with
          the stick as long as possible.

right shoulder is brought forward and the ball shovelled over the opponent to achieve height. This method of passing requires a greater adjustment of body position than the aerial flick, and therefore gives more notice to the opposition that the pass is going to be made.

RECEIVING AND CONTROLLING THE BALL

On receiving the ball, players must gain instant control. The first touch on the ball when receiving it is critical. If the ball bounces off the stick there are increased chances that opponents will have an opportunity to win the ball. If instant control is achieved, the player receiving the ball gains time and space enabling him to choose his pass with greater ease.

When receiving the ball, the stick will either be used in the open or reverse stick position. The method adopted by a player will depend on what action the player has to take next. For example, if a centre half is receiving the ball from the left and wants to pass right, the ball will be received outside the right foot after it has crossed the body enabling the player to move immediately to the right. At all times when receiving the ball players must control the ball in relation to their next move.

Basically, the ball is either received from *in front*, from *the right*, or from *the left*. From the left all passes should be taken with the open stick. From the right passes will be received with both open and reverse stick. From in front as many passes as possible should be taken with the open stick. The method adopted to receive the ball will depend on which area the ball is received from and where the player wishes to pass the ball. When a player is receiving the ball from the right and passing to the left, the best method of receiving the ball will be with the reverse stick in front of the left

foot, thus enabling the player to pass left with the least adjustment and, therefore, saving time.

The action a player takes before receiving the ball will also assist the player to gain good control. The stronger the position a player is in, the more likelihood there is of good control being gained. If the ball is received on the reverse side, it must be moved to the open side – the strong side – as quickly as possible.

From in Front *(Figs 21 & 22)*

Receiving the ball from the front differs on synthetic grass to natural grass. As is seen in Figs 21 and 22 the stick is held almost upright compared with the flatter position of the stick on synthetic grass, where the run of the ball is much more predictable, see Figs 22a and 22b. On synthetic grass the ball is controlled and moved into the next position almost in the same movement.

On natural grass the stick is gripped as for individual ball control, the left hand at the top of the stick and the right hand about halfway, or further, down. The body should be in line with the incoming ball presenting an upright stick which is inclined forwards at the top. The knees are bent and the head is over the ball. If the ball bounces, the whole face of the stick is in position to control the ball. If the stick is diagonally across the body, the area to control the ball is far less.

As soon as the ball is controlled, the body is moved into position to hit or push the ball away, or for the player to move forwards on his own with the ball. If the ball is to be hit or pushed, the left- and right-hand grip must be readjusted for the selected pass.

From the Left *(Figs 23 & 24)*

Vision has already been emphasised as an important part of a player's game. The danger of turning the body to the left when the ball

Fig 21   Body in line with incoming ball;
          eyes watching ball.

Fig 23   Running forward, eyes following
          the ball.

Fig 22   Ball controlled in front of body.

Fig 24   Ball controlled to the right of the body
          to allow forward movement.

approaches a player from his left side is that the player cannot see quickly what is happening on the right-hand side of the pitch. If the player wishes to see what is happening to the right of the field, he must increase his arc of vision. The receiving technique shown in *Figs 23* and *24* will enable the receiver to see more.

The movement to the right having received the ball from the left is enhanced by an adjustment of stick and footwork. If the player receiving is in space and under no pressure, then the method adopted to receive the ball approaching from the left becomes less important. Again, note that the method selected to receive the ball will depend on the circumstances in play at the time.

From the Right *(Figs 25 & 26)*

Passes received from the right will be taken either with the open, or reverse stick. If the open stick is being adopted, the upper body is moved round to get the best view of the incoming ball. Those passes that are being received with the stick in the reverse position will be taken in front or outside the line of the left foot. As described previously, the method of receiving the ball will depend on what the receiver's next move is to be.

Where a wall pass is to be played, the ball will be best received on the open stick. However, if the player receiving wished to play it to the left, the best method of receiving the ball would be with the reverse stick in front of the left foot. For each of these moves the minimum adjustment has to be made by the receiver to make the required pass. Selecting the wrong method of receiving will take longer to perform the pass and therefore increase the

Fig 25   Forward movement maintained, eyes watching the ball.

Fig 26   Stick reversed to control the ball to the left of the body to allow forward movement.

chance of failure.

As the players move into the circle, they should receive the ball in such a way that a shot can be made with the minimum adjustment. Wherever possible, the ball should be received with the open stick, the ball being adjusted quickly ready for a quick shot.

The rules now allow players receiving the ball to have their backs to their opponents, effectively doing away with the advantage rule. However, the receiver must be moving, he cannot stand still with his back to his opponent. On receipt of the ball the player in possession may move either to the right or left effectively shielding the ball.

TACKLING

Tackling is the term used to dispossess an

Fig 27 Player closing down attacker, ready to tackle.

Fig 28 Open side tackle – player moving in, watching the ball.

Fig 29   Tackler moves in with low stick to trap ball.

opponent of the ball, but it requires a more detailed explanation. Tackling should be seen in three phases:

1. Closing down the space available for the opponent.
2. Preparing and moving into a strong tackling position.
3. Tackling and gaining ball possession.

Tackles come within three areas: the tackle in front of the body, the open side tackle and the reverse side tackle. Good footwork is essential to effective tackling. The tackler must be in a strong position from which he can change his position quickly. When making a tackle players must avoid any contact with the opponent's stick before playing the ball. Inevitably there will be clashes of sticks – Umpires will be looking to see that there has been no interference with the opponent's stick in the process of playing the ball.

Closing Down *(Fig 27)*

If an opponent has good control of the ball as he approaches, there is little point in rushing in to tackle and thus creating a situation that the attacker can easily avoid. At the same time, to leave an attacker too much space gives him too many options for passes. The tackler should move in to force the attacker to slow down and only leave passes to the side or back available, at the same time getting into a position ready to tackle as soon as the time is right, i.e. as the opponent's stick moves away from the ball. On artificial grass where the player with the ball may have good close control the defender should look to 'jockey' the attacker away from the area of greatest danger while waiting for the opportune moment to tackle. It is better at times when playing on artificial grass not to tackle at the same time, avoiding any chance of the opponent getting into an attacking position.

Fig 30   Tackler must avoid contact with
          opponent's stick or body prior to
          tackling.

Preparation

The player moving in to tackle must get into a
strong mobile position with the left side forward and the stick in a position from which it
can be moved quickly in to take the ball when
the opportunity arises. From this position, the
tackler can move to his right for an open side
tackle, or to the left for a reverse side tackle. In
both cases the body pivots on the right leg to
move right or left.

In Front of the Body

If an attacker moves in close to the tackler,
coming straight at him, the tackler can play
with both hands on the stick giving a very
strong tackle. As soon as the ball is won, the
tackler must get quickly into the required
passing position. If the attacker is keeping

close control of the ball the tackler will 'jab' at
the ball. As soon as the ball is won the tackler
must get into the strongest possible position
for his next move.

Open Side *(Figs 28 & 29)*

This tackle takes place either as an opponent
moving towards the tackler moves away to
the tackler's right or as the defender is moving
back towards his own goal-line chasing the
attacker.

In the first case, as the attacker moves
away to the tackler's right, the left side is
brought round and the stick placed in a low
position to present as wide a face as possible
to the ball. As soon as the tackle is made, the
right hand is replaced on the stick to give extra
strength for the next move. Making the tackle
with only the left hand on the stick gives the
tackler a longer reach.

Fig 31   A low, strong position, allowing an efficient tackle.

In the second case, when a tackler has to chase the attacker to make the tackle, the stick is again held in the left hand and kept close to the ball to give the attacker the least possible notice of the tackle. If the attempted tackle is preceded by a long swing of the stick, the attacker can easily readjust the position of the ball and avoid the tackle. Again, as soon as the tackle is made, pass the right hand on to the stick to get in as strong a position as possible.

Reverse Side *(Figs 30 & 31)*

The reverse side tackle causes more infringements of the rules than the other tackles. The timing of the tackle and the way the tackler positions his body to make the tackle is very important. Like the open side tackle, it can be performed in two ways.

1. Adjusting from the position adopted in closing the attacker down.
2. In retreat, chasing an attacker in possession of the ball.

In the first instance, as the attacker moves to the tackler's left, the tackler pivots on his right leg to bring his body into a position facing the point at which the tackle will take place. The grip on the stick has to be changed to ensure that the toe of the stick is pointing down, the

Fig 32 Defender waiting for right moment to tackle, when attacker has ball in good control.

flat face of the stick facing the ball. The body must be in a low strong position to give an effective tackling stance.

In the second instance, the angle at which the tackler approaches the attacker will help in making a good tackle. The tackler should attempt to approach the attacker so that, at the point of tackle, the tackler's stick is in front of the ball and not interfering with the attacker's stick. As with the other tackle, the ball must be brought into the strong position and the right hand placed back on the stick as quickly as possible.

Whatever the method of tackling selected in any particular situation, the following elements are particularly important:

1. Patience. Select the right moment for the tackle. Wait rather than hurry.
2. Timing. The tackler must time the moment to move in and win the ball, often when the attacker takes his stick away from the ball.

3. Strength. Always get into the strongest possible position to tackle.
4. Footwork. Do not be caught square; always be in a mobile position.

BEATING AN OPPONENT

Beating an opponent is an extension of individual ball control. It is the ability to move a defender out of position to create space to take the ball past him, at the same time understanding that as a player is forced to move there are areas in which that player is more vulnerable than others. Before describing the various methods of beating an opponent, where possession of the ball is retained, it must be remembered that very often the best method of beating an opponent is to pass the ball.

In attempting to beat an opponent either on

the opponent's open or reverse side, players must realise the importance of the following:

1. Close control of the ball, allowing good vision.
2. The ability to move the opponent and create the space to pass the player, requiring a *change of direction*.
3. The ability to *change pace*, both to slow down and to accelerate.
4. The ability to move in behind defenders after beating them (cutting the player out) to ensure they do not have a second attempt to tackle.

Methods of Beating an Opponent

The Approach

As the attacker approaches the defender, the ball is well out in front of the body ensuring that the attacker has a good view of the defender. Again note the importance of good vision in preparing to move to the left (to the opponent's open side) or to the right (to the opponent's reverse side).

The recent change in the rules now allows the receiver of the ball to place his body between the opponent and the ball, providing the receiver does not stand still. This creates a further method of beating an opponent. The ball can be laid off to a supporting player, or the player who has received the ball can shield it from the defender as he moves away.

Reverse Side (Figs 33 to 35)

The initial move by the attacker must be to move the defender to his right, thus wrong-footing him. This change of direction must be a definite movement of ball and body. The defender has to move or the attacker will continue along the new line. This move must

also be made early; if the attacker gets within the stick reach of the defender before making his move, the defender can reach the ball without having to move. Players often get too close to defenders before changing direction.

Having moved the defender to his right, the ball is moved across the front of the defender. When moving the ball across to the defender's reverse side, the attacker must again ensure that the ball is played across the defender away from the defender's stick.

The third move is where the attacker accelerates the ball and himself into the space behind the defender. The importance of the acceleration cannot be underestimated. If the attacker is slow in this third stage, it gives the defender the opportunity to turn and make a reverse side tackle.

Open Side (Figs 36 to 38)

In this instance, the attacker's first move is to change direction, taking the defender to the defender's left. The ball is then pulled across in front of the defender, wide of the defender's open stick. How wide the ball is taken will depend on the speed of recovery of the defender. The attacker must be prepared to go very wide, taking the ball reverse stick and well to his left. Finally the attacker accelerates in behind the defender. If the attacker has taken the ball very wide and one handed to his reverse side, he must get the right hand back onto the stick as quickly as possible.

Cutting the Defender Out

Having come back into the original line of approach, the attacker cuts the defender out and reduces the possibility of the defender getting a second chance to dispossess the attacker. If the attacker does not come back onto the original line, the defender can recover and make a further attempt to dispossess the attacker.

Fig 33 Beating opponent on his reverse side –
move opponent to his right.

Fig 35 Move quickly behind opponent and
accelerate away.

Fig 34 Switch ball to opponent's reverse side.

Fig 36 Beating opponent on his open side –
move opponent to his left.

Fig 37   Move ball wide to opponent's open side.

Fig 38   Move in quickly behind opponent.

GOALKEEPING

Goalkeeping is an exciting specialist job, one that can result in dramatic saves which keep a team in a game. Bravery, as demonstrated by Ian Taylor in the Great Britain goal in the 1984 Los Angeles Olympics, is an essential characteristic that all good goalkeepers must possess along with good judgement, good positioning, fast reactions and good technique. In addition, goalkeepers must maintain a high degree of flexibility, strength, stamina and concentration. Above all, they must have confidence.

Goalkeeping requires good basic techniques on which each goalkeeper builds his own style. Coaches and young goalkeepers must be cautious about attempting the style of goalkeeping adopted by experienced top flight keepers unless the young goalkeeper is properly equipped. Goalkeeping equipment is expensive; however, no player should be asked to keep goal unless they have the type of equipment described in chapter 8.

Goalkeeping is a highly specialised job, the changes in the equipment worn by goalkeepers has enabled them to develop a whole new style of goalkeeping. The full protection of the body means they can lie flat on the ground, presenting a complete barrier to protect the goal, for example, at penalty corners, or they can be on their feet moving quickly around the circle to challenge an incoming forward. However, if a goalkeeper is going to go down in this way the ability to get up quickly to protect the goal in the standing position becomes very important. Goalkeepers have to develop the strength and agility to be down one moment and standing up in the next instance.

Goalkeeping requires specialised coaching and the Hockey Association now provides specific goalkeeper coaches for clubs, including John Hurst who was himself

Fig 39   Goalkeeper moves across towards
         the ball.

Fig 40   Goalkeeper saves and clears ball at the
         same time.

Fig 41 Goalkeeper clearing ball away from
main area to the point of least danger.

an outstanding England and Great Britain goalkeeper.

Preparing to Save

In preparing to control a ball or play it away, the goalkeeper must be balanced and able to move quickly in whatever direction the circumstances demand. The save used by the goalkeeper will depend on two particular factors:

1. The speed of the shot – a fast shot will rebound further than a slow shot.
2. The position of opponents – the save must be made away from incoming attackers using the momentum of the ball to make the save and clearance in one movement.

While preparing to clear the ball the goalkeeper has to be aware of the opponents' positions to ensure the clearance does not provide the opposition with the chance to continue their attack.

Saving and Clearing

If the goalkeeper is not under pressure from other players he will be able to block the shot at goal and then clear the ball with his feet or stick to the area of least danger, hoping to initiate an attack.

The goalkeeper ensures he has a balanced position with the pads together, knees forward, ensuring that the ball is played with the instep of either foot with the weight going forward as the ball is played on to the

Fig 42 *Goalkeeper saving the ball, his position enabling him to cut out crosses. Note the defender covering.*

saving foot.

The ball being played to a point selected for the clearance, the save and clear is made in one movement. The head must be brought forward over the saving leg to ensure that the ball is kept on the ground. The lifted ball could be dangerous and result in the umpire awarding a penalty corner to the opposition. The make-up of the goalkeeper's kickers and pads provide the rebound surface for the ball to be cleared well away from the goal and the defensive danger area.

To ensure that the goalkeeper is able to move quickly to intercept shots he must be very agile and quick on his feet, being able to save a shot, recover and save again in quick succession. If a goalkeeper clears the ball but has his weight on the non-saving leg he will find he is falling away from the save and consequently less able to prepare for the next shot. The goalkeeper must attack the ball going into the save and through the line bringing the weight forward. Practices must be designed to enable the goalkeeper to perform the movements involved. To do this goalkeepers require individual training where

*Fig 43   Goalkeeper moves across to block shot
with hand.*

the service they are given is designed especially for the aspect of goalkeeping they are practising.

The equipment goalkeepers now wear enables them to save the ball with virtually any part of the body. At Penalty Corners goalkeepers go down to present a complete barrier to the ball which is fine providing other players in the defence are ready to clear any ball that rebounds off, or is saved by, the goalkeeper.

Clearing and Saving with the Stick (Fig 42)

While goalkeepers should attempt to save with the pads initially, there will be times when the stick has to be used, for example when having blocked a shot, the goalkeeper does not have time to kick the ball away. The ball should be cleared either to the left or right,

away from the areas covered by opponents. The stick is used as an extension of the right arm to make saves which are wide of the goalkeeper's reach, and out of range to save with the pads.

The goalkeeper should avoid playing the ball intentionally over the goal-line, as this will result in a penalty corner being awarded against his team. Only in an absolute emergency should such action be taken.

Saving with the Hand (Fig 43)

The left hand will be used to save shots wide of the goalkeeper's left side, and high and wide to the goalkeeper's right. In making these saves the goalkeeper must avoid propelling the ball forwards, which infringes the rules. He may move the hand into line to save the ball, allowing the ball to deflect off the hand. If the ball is coming high and straight at

Fig 44   *Goalkeeper in position of readiness,
guarding near post. Note the balanced
position with pads together and knees
forward.*

the goalkeeper, he must ensure the flat of the
hand is presented to the ball and that the ball
drops down, and is not propelled forwards.

Positioning *(Fig 44)*

The goalkeeper must attempt to maintain a
position between the ball and the centre of the
goal, where he narrows down the angle available to the attacker. As a player comes into
the circle the goalkeeper moves a few paces
off his line to narrow the available angle for the
attacker to shoot at goal. When the ball is
passed, the goalkeeper moves quickly to take
up a new position to cover the new area. At all
times, the goalkeeper must be aware of his
position relative to the ball and the centre of

the goal, particularly at penalty corners.

The goalkeeper should be adjusting his position at all times in relation to the position of the ball, moving around an imaginary arc in front of the circle. When a goalkeeper is confronted by a solo attacker, positioning is most important. The goalkeeper should close the space down between himself and the attacker, and try to force the attacker to go to the goalkeeper's open side (his stronger side).

To be effective, the goalkeeper must have the flexibility to reach wide shots, and strength and speed to get back onto his feet and into the ready position. Goalkeepers come into the game for short periods, often after what may be a long period of inactivity when the game is at the far end of the pitch. Concentration, therefore, becomes very important. The goalkeeper should follow the game throughout, adjusting his position all the time in relation to the ball and the centre of the goal. When play is in, or near the goalkeeper's circle he must be in full control of the situation. The goalkeeper has the best view of play, and must ensure that he always has a clear view of the ball. Sensible calling is helpful to other players who may not have such a good view of play.

2 Team Play

PRINCIPLES

The first reaction of many teachers and coaches when discussing the development of team play is to think of the full eleven-a-side game. This is a mistake. Much has to be done before players are ready to take part in the full game.

Hockey contains two clearly defined phases: *attack* and *defence*. As possession is won or lost, the emphasis changes and players have to react accordingly. Within the attacking and defending phases the skills must be developed. These skills are best developed in game-like activities and small team games. Tactical and skill learning must be linked where ever possible.

1. **Passing**. Is the ball being passed to retain possession, to relieve pressure, or to penetrate the opposition defence?
2. **The pass**. What type of pass is required at any given time to retain possession – a short push pass, a long hit pass or a wall pass?
3. **Movement off the ball**. Are players moving to support the player with the ball, or to cover a group of players?
4. **Marking**. Has the player marking positioned himself to see his opponent, or to see the ball?
5. **Attack to defence**. What action should a particular player take at the moment possession of the ball is lost?

These are only five examples of the skills that have to be learned and understood. If introduced in isolation to the game these are value-less, they must be learned in game-like activities as described in the progressive practices section in Chapter 6. Learning must start the first time the player is introduced to the game – in the first coaching session.

The five stages of learning described in the joint publication of the Hockey Association and the All England Womens Hockey Association, *A Common Approach to the Introduction of Hockey*, are an excellent guide to the development of team play. In essence the five stages are:

Stage 1 Skills learning.
Stage 2 Small team games.
Stage 3 Mini-hockey.
Stage 4 Seven-a-side hockey.
Stage 5 Eleven-a-side hockey.

The aim in this chapter is to outline what players should learn in preparation for the full game. The three aspects of play are listed below.

Aim

In attack : to score goals.
In defence : to prevent goals.

Style of Play

In attack : fluid and inventive.
In defence : disciplined and organised.

Principles of Play

In attack : width, support, possession, speed, penetration, mobility.

In defence : depth, cover, speed, security, delay, restriction of space.

The details set out here should be introduced to players as soon as possible; they are not details that are left to the game. The simplest skill practice, if it is well structured can have an important influence on the understanding of the principles of play.

To perform effectively in the full game players must have a full understanding of the styles of play required at differing stages in a game and in the different areas of the pitch. The hockey pitch can be divided into three areas, as shown in *Fig 45*.

Defence Area

Opposition in Possession

The aim is to defend this area, particularly the circle, by restricting the area available to the opposition. Mark those opposition players in close proximity to the ball, and cover if the ball is away from your area, while waiting to mark when the ball is transferred to your part of the field. To achieve this type of play good *organisation* and *discipline* are required. Players must do the job they have been asked to do. Players who 'ball watch' often fail to mark their opponent effectively.

Your Team in Possession

The attack must start now. This will require movement off the ball to create space for those in possession to make safe passes and move into the build-up area. The ball must be played quickly but safely out of the defence area. Players who continue to mark their opponents once their side is in possession will not be helping their team to make passes.

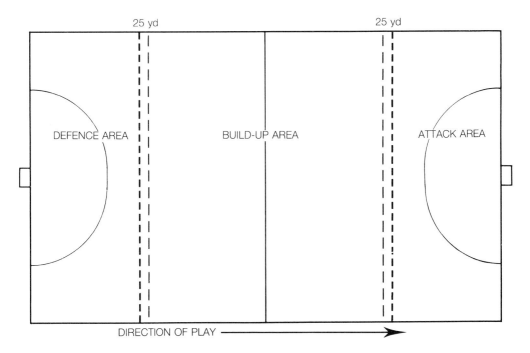

Fig 45

Build-up Area

Opposition in Possession

All the remarks applied to the defence area are relevant in the build-up area. The crucial additional factors are the speed at which players move and where they move to at the moment the opposition wins the ball, when attack turns to defence.

The way players react to the changed situation will depend on the style of defence that the team has adopted: whether man-to-man marking, zonal marking or a combination of the two are being employed. Often opponents gain advantage at this stage of a game because mid-field players and forwards do not adopt their defensive role immediately. The change from attack to defence requires a change in mental attitude to the game situation. Slow decision making and reaction at this stage can result in opponents putting unnecessary pressure on the defence.

Your Team in Possession

In the build-up area the retention of possession is essential if goal-scoring chances are going to be created. Creative and inventive play leads to opportunities to penetrate the attacking area and create goal-scoring chances. The speed with which the ball is moved through the build-up area will depend on the distribution, organisation and effectiveness of the opponents' defence. The quicker the ball is moved through the build-up area the less time the opponents have to cover and close down spaces. However, if the opposition is well organised when an attack is mounted it will take longer to build a successful attack; openings will have to be created through which play can penetrate.

To create openings it will often be necessary to change the point of attack, to play the ball wide using the width of the field to spread the opposition defence. Movement off the ball to support the player with the ball or to draw opponents away from areas of the field, will create opportunities and enable a team to retain effective possession. Effective possession is when a team keeps possession and at the same time moves forwards to penetrate the attack area. Possession can easily be maintained by moving the ball square and back, but this type of play, unless it is being used for a specific purpose (for example, to draw the opponents' defenders forward and out of their defending area), rarely results in penetration.

When moving from the build-up area to the attack area it is important that players get used to playing the ball into space behind their opponents to give their own team members the opportunity to get away from defenders and gain possession of the ball.

Attack Area

Opposition in Possession

Defence in the opposition's circle is an aspect of the game that some young players find difficult to grasp. A team starts to defend as soon as possession is lost wherever play is on the field. Every player has a role to play in defence. The front line players have a vital role in attempting to delay the opposition clearing the ball, thus giving players in mid-field and defence time to take up their defensive positions. The forwards should harry and chase the player in possession, forcing him to make errors, anticipating his passes and attempting to intercept the ball as it is played out of defence. Forwards who do not effectively play their part in defence enable the opposition to clear the ball quickly which often results in pressure being put on players in mid-field or defence.

Your Team in Possession

As the ball moves into the attack area players should act quickly, either in solo efforts or in support of other players. Once in the circle, attackers must be prepared to shoot, and other players should be ready to play a rebound off the goalkeeper's pads back into goal.

When attacking players move into pre-planned positions for a purpose, the movement is called a 'set piece in open play'. It requires tight planning and split-second timing but will result in more goal-scoring chances. More risks can be taken in the attacking area. Players need to vary their movements and be mobile and fluid in their play to create problems for the defending team.

Elements of Play

In the previous sections a number of points have come to light which should be thoroughly understood and implemented. These are:

1. Restricting the area available to the opposition.
2. Movement off the ball.
3. Retention of possession.
4. Creative and inventive play.
5. In attack, be mobile and fluid.
6. In defence, harry and chase.
7. Support in attack.
8. Defend as soon as possession is lost.

These elements of play are equally applicable to mini-hockey, seven-a-side hockey and the full game. The sophistication of their performance will vary considerably from the learner to the high-class player. Understood well they will lead to a far greater ability to 'read the game' and will assist individuals to mould into effective team units.

Practices

Small team games are ideal for introducing the principles of play. The coach, in selecting a small team game to be used to cover a particular tactic or skill, has to decide if players will be concentrated in attack or defence. This decision will determine the type of practices used. If aspects of attack are the prime object the coach will select practices where numerical superiority is given to the attacking group. Defending practices will have a far greater emphasis on each individual's responsibility within the group. These practices should progress from groups of three to larger groups working together.

To help groups to appreciate discipline and organisation players should work to patterns, the three-player triangle being the starting point. When players start to see their responsibility to each other they can then move on to multi-triangle patterns, as described below.

In *Fig 46*, the opposition (O) are attacking; X has the ball. B is marking X. A is in a covering position while C has moved back a little to give cover and yet be in a position to move forward to mark Z when the ball is played square. When the ball is played away from the player B is marking he moves back to give cover in width, but is still in a position to move in to mark X if the ball is played back. As the ball is switched A adjusts his covering position at the back of the triangle. Should Y receive the ball and come forwards through the middle, A is available to engage Y. Providing A, B and C remain disciplined and organised, adjusting their positions to the point of attack, they will form a sound defence. The shape of the triangle will change according to where the ball is positioned. The actual distances each player has to travel are small to retain an organised pattern.

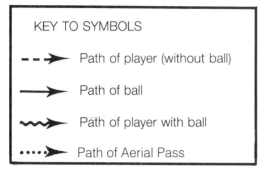

KEY TO SYMBOLS

- - ➤   Path of player (without ball)

———➤   Path of ball

∿∿➤   Path of player with ball

••••➤   Path of Aerial Pass

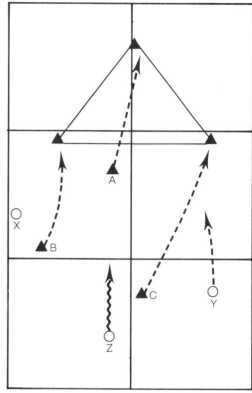

Fig 47

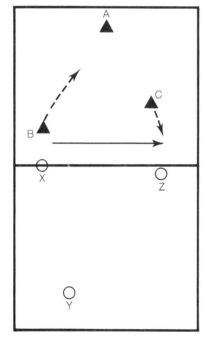

Fig 46

To make the above practice more difficult, the playing area can be increased in size to six grids and conditions imposed on play to ensure that the specific aspects of defensive play are emphasised. The attacking players are allowed to be as fluid and inventive as they wish, but the defenders must retain their pattern and organisation, in other words they must be well disciplined.

In *Fig 47*, C loses possession to Z near the opposition's goal-line. Immediately this happens C's team must form a triangle in their half, ready to readjust their positions. The condition is that they must form a triangle in their own half on the goal side of their opponents. By imposing this condition the coach has ensured that the mental process on losing possession immediately changes from attacking to defensive thinking.

Once players understand this relationship in a simple triangle they can move on to patterns involving four players, taking the diamond as the basic form. In the diamond pattern players have a responsibility to two triangles.

In *Fig 48*, the basic diamond pattern is shown with four players, A, B, C and D. This is the

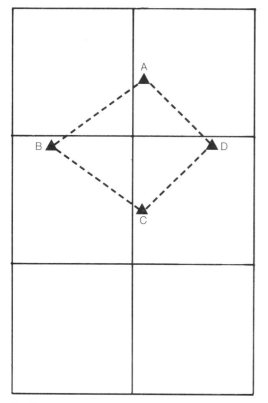

Fig 48

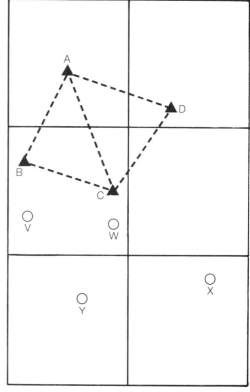

Fig 49

defensive base pattern. As the opposition moves the ball to one side of the playing area the relationship of the players to each other changes.

In *Fig 49*, the triangle of players marking the area of greatest danger is formed by A, B and C. B and C are marking with A covering. D's relationship to triangle DAC and to player X is important. D is covering A and C for any diagonal pass that may be made between the two players, but is still in a position to move to X should the ball be switched to that side, when D and C would be marking with A covering them, and B moving to cover A and C.

This organisation results in depth and cover being given and it delays the opposition's attack. By starting to introduce these aspects of play with small numbers, players gain a far greater understanding of their application. This can be developed through the small sided games, mini-hockey and seven-a-side hockey. If the principles of play are clearly understood at this stage then the full game will be far easier to master. These activities, using small numbers to develop an understanding of attacking and defending principles, give players concentrated practice on specific aspects of play. As players move through small team games increasing their number to the full eleven-a-side game the principles of play remain the same but each player's involvement becomes more complex.

SKILLS APPLIED TO TEAM PLAY

The general aims, styles and principles of play have been described. To put these successfully into operation players have to apply the skills of the game. To illustrate this an actual playing situation is shown in *Fig 50*.

While coaches might claim the positioning of players could be slightly different, this exam-ple is used to demonstrate the skills. When considering the skills set out in this example, coaches should observe the following points:

There may be some confusion caused in coaches' minds with the use of playing position names in diagrams in this section and those that follow. I refer to my midfield players' positions as Inside Forwards and Centre Half as I believe this creates a more attacking attitude in their minds. The inside forwards see themselves as forward play-

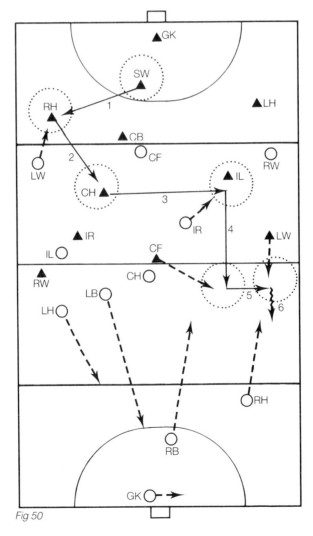

Fig 50

ers. The term Midfield players often takes an element of attack out of a player's mind. The terms Right Half and Left Half are used as opposed to Right and Left Defender. However, the terms Centre Back and Sweeper are used. The roles these players play will vary but the phraseology used is intended to create an attacking attitude in players' minds.

Pass 1 (SW to RH)

1. Is the SW's method of passing to the RH effective?
2. Has the RH moved to assist the passer?
3. Has the opposition LW moved in to close down the space available for the RH?
4. Is the way the RH receives the ball assisting him to make *Pass 2* to the CH?

Pass 2 (RH to CH)

1. In receiving the ball has the CH given himself full vision of what is available, particularly in preparation to make *Pass 3*?
2. To make a square pass to retain possession and change the point of attack has the IL positioned himself to assist the next passer?

Pass 3 (CH to IL)

1. This must be square because a diagonal pass forwards would be intercepted by the opposition IR.
2. In receiving the ball, has the IL positioned himself so he can control the ball and immediately play the ball forwards into space for the CF to move on to?

Pass 4 (IL to CF)

1. To receive the pass the CF has to get away from the close marking of the opposition's CH. This will involve timing his run for the ball and in so doing trying to wrong foot the CH, and changing pace by accelerating away from the defender.
2. As the CF moves in to receive the ball the opposition CH will be attempting to tackle the CF and the opposition RB will be moving in to close the space down. The CF, therefore, may have to control the ball and immediately pass to the LW.

Pass 5 (CF to LW)

1. The LW must not have moved too far forward to ensure the pass can be played square. A diagonal pass would give the opposition RH a chance of possession.
2. The LW, on receiving the ball, must continue his forward movement to beat his opponent, the RH, and attack the opponent's defence are with a solo run.

Each skill is identified by a broken circle and includes receipt of the ball. However, each method of receiving can be very different. Practices involving receiving the ball must have this game-like element in them. Coaches must create practice situations that give the players the experience they will need in the game.

The skills of hockey can be highlighted under the following headings:

1. Passing the ball.
2. Receiving the ball.
3. Movement off the ball.
4. Beating an opponent.
5. Losing a close marking opponent.
6. Vision.
7. Winning the ball.
8. Marking and cover.
9. Counter attack.

Each of these skills requires the use of particular techniques in differing skill situations. In the game situation described above a number of methods of receiving the ball are used, and the passes will be pushes and hits executed slightly differently from each other. Each of the skills listed above has to be subdivided and developed so that players in the game can select the correct method to deal with a particular situation. Players must react to a problem immediately to ensure that they cope with that problem effectively. To ensure players have full knowledge of what is happening around them they must be constantly aware of the positioning of their own team and the opponents. Their decision on actions to be taken will be based on this knowledge. Adopting the incorrect method of receiving the ball, for example, can often delay the next pass being made and give the opponent the opportunity to tackle or intercept the pass.

Passing

Players must understand why they use a particular pass and how it should be executed. The passes most often used are the square pass, the through pass, the back pass, the wall pass and the aerial pass.

Square Pass (Figs 51 to 53)

The square pass can be used to retain possession and to relieve pressure.

In *Fig 51*, the RH has moved back and square to enable the SW to pass, so that his team can retain possession and relieve the pressure caused by the IL moving in towards the top of the circle.

The square pass can also be used to change the point of attack from one part of the field to another, where the playing area may be less congested and, therefore, offers a better chance of an attack being developed. The pass should be played very firmly with either a hit or a push to ensure that the ball travels quickly, giving the receiver as much time and space in which to control the ball as possible.

Another use for the square pass is to create a better opening for another player.

In *Fig 52*, the IL has moved forward with the ball to engage the SW and has given a short square pass to his CF who attempts a shot at goal. The IL has drawn the sweeper to make the pass more effective.

Lastly, the square pass can be used as part of a combined movement where the player making the pass moves to receive a through pass.

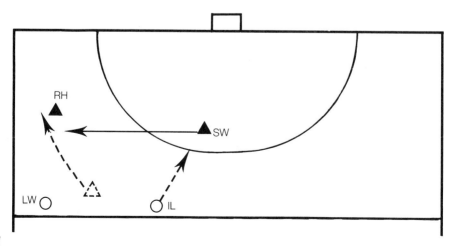

Fig 51

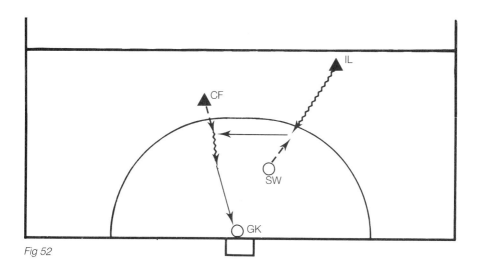

Fig 52

In *Fig 53*, the IR has moved with the ball to draw the LH and has played the ball square to his RW, moving diagonally to receive the through pass down the line.

In the square pass examples, a diagonal pass would have given the opponent an

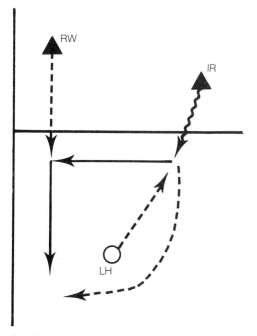

Fig 53

opportunity to intercept and would have made the receiver's task much more difficult.

Through Pass (Figs 54 to 59)

The through pass is used to penetrate opposition lines whether they be in the defence area, the build-up area or the attack area. It is a pass that is often played poorly because players do not give enough thought to the use of space and to the position of markers in relation to the person who is to receive the pass. The pass is too often played diagonally and thus within reach of opponents.

A through pass is either played to a player or into space for a player to move on to, the latter being something that young players find difficult to master. A through ball is often difficult to collect as the receiver may be closely marked by an opponent.

In the defence and build-up areas, through passes must be played so that possession is retained. In the attack area, while the prime object must be to retain possession (otherwise goals cannot be scored), greater chances may be taken, in the hope that a player may be able to reach the ball and shoot at goal, or centre the ball into the circle.

Team Play

The following two examples show successful and unsuccessful through passes.

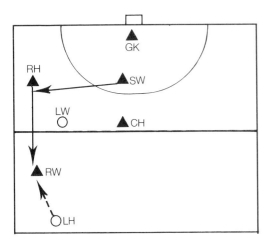

Fig 54

In *Fig 54*, the RH, after receiving a pass from the SW, has played a good through pass to the RW down the reverse side of the LW who has moved in-field.

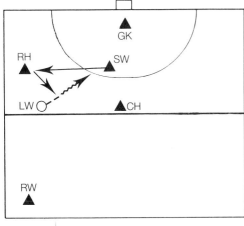

Fig 55

In *Fig 55*, the RH has attempted a diagonal through pass to the CH which has been intercepted by the LW, who then runs with the ball

and immediately attacks the sweeper and the circle at a time when the defence has little cover.

Coaches have to assess why the RH made this mistake. The likelihood is that the initial method of receiving the ball did not widen the RH's vision enough for him to be able to play the ball down the line before pressure was put on him. To create passing awareness and overcome the situation shown in the second example, 3 v I practices with movements similar to these should be used.

In the mid-field, diagonal through passes can be successful once players have created space and have an understanding of the pace at which the ball should be played. The straight through pass will also be employed to penetrate into space behind opponents. The two examples below show how these passes may be employed.

(Fig 56) The initial pass from the LH to the CH is good. The CH immediately sees a space in front of the IR into which he plays a diagonal through pass for the IR to run on to. The line and pace of the pass is such that the IR moving forwards can control the ball and assess what his next move should be before the opponent's defence has changed its balance and the LB has moved forward to close down on the IR.

In *Fig 57*, if the CH plays the same pass to the IR as in the example above, the IL would intercept, so a square pass to the RH then a straight through pass into a space for the IR to move on to must be played. This has the effect of penetrating the space behind the opposition's IL and gives the IR the opportunity to set up an attack with the RW.

The same result has been achieved in both examples but the method of implementing the play was different because the CH had good vision and read the situation well. The secret of success in these two examples has been

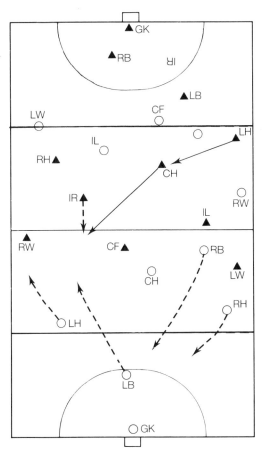

Fig 56

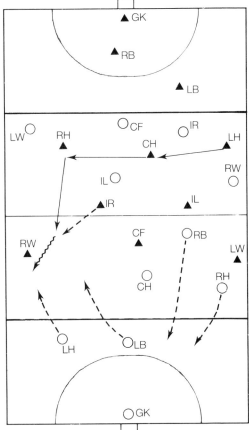

Fig 57

the speed of ball movement creating time and space for the through pass to be made. Had either the CH or RH run with the ball they would have given the opposition's defence time to close down the areas into which the through pass could be played.

The outcome of the moves described above is that the through ball can be played in the attack area, again using a diagonal or straight through pass as shown in *Fig 58*.

The available space for the attack to be made is behind the opposition's LH and LB, so the IR plays a diagonal through pass into that space for the RW to run on to and attack the goal-line.

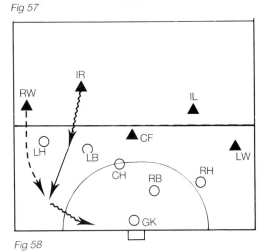

Fig 58

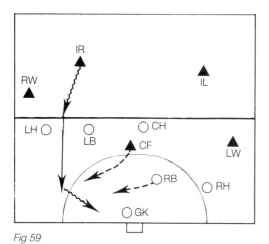

Fig 59

In *Fig 59*, the opposition's LH is further away from the RW, and the CF has got on to the goal-side of the opposition CH. The IR plays a straight through pass into space for the CF to run diagonally on to and attack the goal.

Whereas a square pass can be hit or pushed with considerable power to the receiving player, giving him added time and space to receive the ball, the through pass has to be carefully judged. The speed of the player receiving the ball and the direction the ball is played must be carefully assessed by the passer. The receiving player and the ball must arrive at the point of control together to give the receiver time to control the ball before he is challenged by an opponent.

Back Pass (Figs 60 to 62)

The back pass is made to relieve pressure, maintain possession and to give a better placed player a chance to play the ball to mount an attack from a different point. Young players are often reluctant to back pass as their initial rule for attack is to plough forwards, which may result in possession being lost.

The following three examples demonstrate how the back pass can be used effectively. In the first example *(Fig 60)* the LH is under considerable pressure from the opposition RW and IR who have cut down his free space and positioned themselves to intercept any pass made forwards. The LH, therefore, checks his forward movement and passes the ball back to the SW who has moved into a

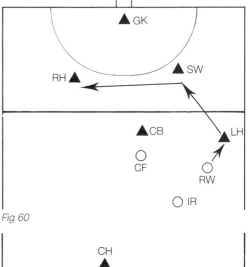

Fig 60

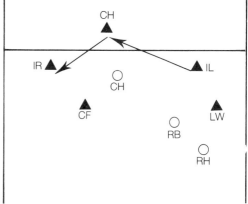

Fig 61

good supporting position. The SW then uses the RH to move the ball away from the congested area for an attack to start on the right.

In the second example *(Fig 61)* the CH is used by the IL to transfer the ball to the IR where a square pass would be intercepted.

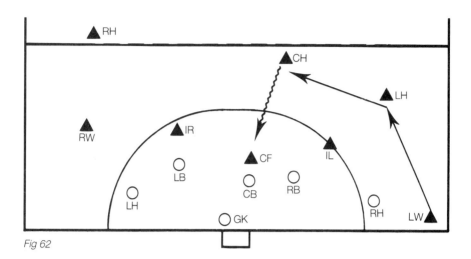

Fig 62

This combination of passes is often referred to as a 'dog-leg' pass.

The third example *(Fig 62)* shows a playing situation which often causes attack problems. The LW has worked the ball down into the attacking left-hand corner of the field. The defence have passes across the circle covered but a back pass to the supporting LH gives an opportunity for the ball to be transferred to the CH, who can attack the circle or switch the ball to the right-hand side of the pitch. The combination of these passes is likely to prove more successful than an attempt at centring, which has little chance of penetrating the opposition defence.

Wall Pass (Figs 63 & 64)

A wall pass is when a player with the ball plays it to a second player who gives an immediate first time return pass. It is used in any area of the field, but if played unsuccessfully in the defence area it can lead to dangerous counter-attacks.

In *Fig 63* the RH moving forwards is blocked by the opposition LW. The IR has positioned himself so that the RH can play a wall pass off the IR and move forwards into attack. The opposition's LW and IL are beaten by the wall pass and the RH has the chance to move into attack.

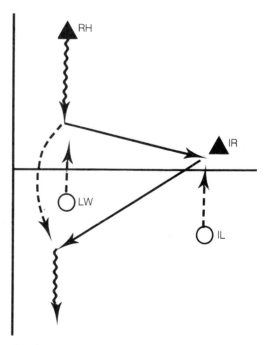

Fig 63

In Fig 64, the LW has played the wall pass off the IL to get behind the RH and into a position to attack the circle.

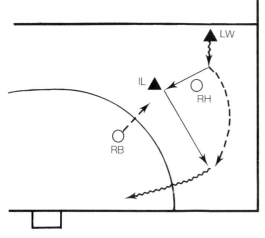

Fig 64

The angle at which both parts of the wall pass are played is vital to its success. The first pass must be given so that the return can be made immediately. If it is played to the IR's right-hand side (as in the first example) or the IL's left-hand side (as in the second example) an immediate return pass becomes impossible. The second pass has to be played so that its angle and speed are such that the receiver can continue his forward movement without checking. The angle the second pass is played at must put the ball out of the opponent's reach.

Aerial Pass (Fig 65)

The aerial pass, as the name suggests, is played over the opponents' heads and is best used when moving out of defence to relieve pressure and from the midfield areas into attack. Care must be taken not to contravene the rules by playing the ball in the air into the opponents' circle. It is important that the aerial pass is not wasted by playing it into crowded areas or causing

dangerous play, either when the ball is being lifted or when it is landing. The pass is most effectively executed when it is put into space behind defenders for attackers to run on to. More often than not this is a long pass, something over 20 metres, but the short-lifted aerial pass of about 10 metres is being used as players become more proficient at performing this skill.

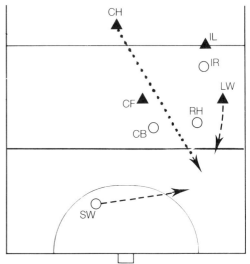

Fig 65

Fig 65 shows a long pass played by the CH from his own half into a space for the LW. This pass has the advantage of drawing the opposition SW out of the centre of the field, and giving the LW the chance to make a solo run or to centre the ball into the circle. The choice made by the LW will depend on how the defence covers and what position his own team members take up.

The types of passes described above are best practised in small sided games. When practising passing and attacking activity, it is important that the attackers have numerical superiority (for example, 4 v 2 in six grid squares). While giving the attackers the advantage in number, it is important to give the two defenders a realistic task in the activity. For example, a condition may be imposed that the four players in possession must make four consecutive passes before attempting a shot at goal. This ensures that they create passing opportunities and retain possession before attempting to score – a good mixture of build-up and attacking play. Their movement off the ball to create passing opportunities becomes very important. The two defenders attempt to intercept the passes and win the ball. Having gained possession they can immediately play the ball over a line to score a goal. Giving the defenders this task has the added advantage of making the attackers realise that when possession is lost they must cover to stop the other team scoring. From the 4 v 2 practice the coach can increase numbers to 6 v 3 with a goalkeeper and then to equal sides.

These passes are going to be used whatever the eventual playing formation chosen for a team; they are part of the repertoire of a good hockey player and should be practised in small groups where individual involvement is far greater than in a game. Where passing has caused a breakdown in tactical play, the coach can isolate the group involved and allow them to overcome their weaknesses in a practice relevant to the game movements in the area of the pitch where the breakdown occurred.

Receiving *(Fig 66)*

Having learned the skills of receiving the ball, players must learn to select the method best suited to a particular situation in the game. Selecting the correct method of receiving the ball is critical to having good vision of play and to the effectiveness of the pass to be made subsequently.

Positioning before receiving assists a player to follow his control of the ball with a good pass. Good footwork beforehand is essential.

The method of receiving must be relevant to what is to be done next. Players must be able to receive the ball from a wide area. This area may be subdivided in five smaller areas as shown.

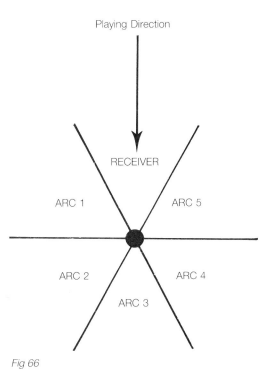

Fig 66

Arc 1

Passes coming from the right diagonally behind the receiver. For passes that are going to be played square or straight forward, or within that area, the ball is best received with the open stick or reverse stick to the right of the body. For passes that are going to be played to the left of the body the ball is best received with the reverse stick in front of the body, thus allowing the ball to travel further before the point of control. The distribution direction of the ball, therefore, determines the point of control.

Arc 2

Any pass to be played back into the area or straight ahead will be controlled with the open stick; any ball to be played on the left of the area should be controlled on the reverse side.

Arc 3

Any ball received within this arc should if possible be controlled with the open stick. The body should be moved to avoid having to control the ball on the reverse side except in an emergency, when there is not time to move the body into position.

Arcs 4 & 5

All passes from these areas will be received on the open stick. The point of control will be determined by the subsequent action to be taken. If the ball is to be returned into areas to the left of the receiver, the ball will be controlled in front of the left foot or between the line of the feet. If the eventual pass is to be made forwards or to the right side of the body, the ball must be controlled in front of or outside the line of the right foot; in other words, it must be allowed to pass across in front of the body before being controlled.

Arc 6

The recent change in the obstruction rule has allowed a player in any arc, but particularly players receiving a pass in Arc 6, to have their backs to their opponents, thus shielding the ball. The rules relating to the movement of the player when receiving are important. Providing the receiver is moving all the time he may keep his body between the ball and the defender. If the receiver moves in to receive the ball in front of the defender and stands still he is then obstructing.

Movement off the Ball
(Figs 67 to 71)

Players' movement off the ball in its simplest form can be regarded in two ways:

1. Movement into a position to receive a pass from another player (support).
2. Movement from an area taking an opponent away thus creating space for a pass to be made, or creating a space into which one of your own team can move.

It is important that players learn to make these movements before passes are made – this creates space for the passer of the ball to use. They *must not* wait for something to happen then move. *Move and make it happen.*

In *Fig 67*, the RH has moved forwards to support the IR and make a square pass possible.
In *Fig 68*, the RW has moved in-field to create space for the RH to move forwards to receive a pass from the IR and attack through the

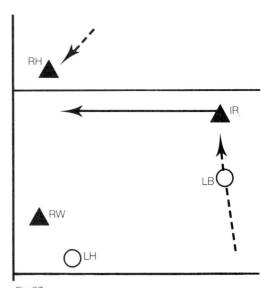

Fig 67

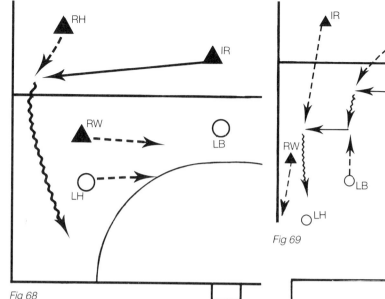

Fig 68

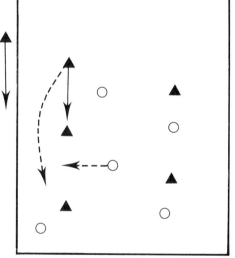

Fig 69

space the RW has created. This move is known as an overlap.

In attack, players should be looking to move off the ball in ways that are going to surprise their opponents and create situations that give numerical superiority in areas of the field, particularly the attacking area which puts the opponent's defence under pressure.

A less common movement off the ball is the loop, where a player moves round behind a team member across the field. This move often causes problems to a defence as it creates numerical superiority on the side of the field that the looping players are moving to.

In *Fig 69*, the IL has passed the ball to the CF and moved round behind him creating a 2 v 1 situation against the opposition LB. The CF makes a return pass to the IL and then moves to his left taking the CH with him, creating space for the attack to take place. The RW moves forward giving a 2 v 1 against the defending LH. This also creates a 3 v 2 situation against the opposition LH and LB.

Conditioned games are ideal for improving players' awareness of the possibilities of overlapping or looping. In 5 v 5 or 6 v 6 games players having made a pass have to move beyond the receiver of the pass.

Fig 70

In *Fig 70*, an attacking player has played the ball forward and made an overlap. The defender has moved across to challenge the attacking player, who must now decide whether to give a return pass, move with the ball himself or change the point of attack. In *Fig 71* the left side opposition player has passed square, looped behind the receiver and received a return pass. He then moves forward with the ball and passes it out to the opposition player on the right and com-

51

mences his second run to go past the receiver.

When making an overlap run or a loop, players must ensure that they avoid committing a third party offence by obstructing. In *Fig 71* if the first loop had been made between the defender and the attacking player, a third party obstruction could have occurred.

When overlapping or looping occurs, a team runs the risk of a movement breakdown with other players not providing cover. Players must be aware of the game as a whole, be able to read the game, and anticipate where areas of danger require covering.

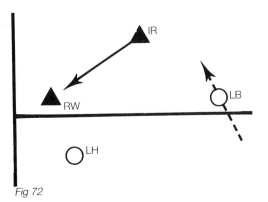

Fig 72

In *Fig 72*, the iR has passed the ball to the RW who is closely marked and likely to be tackled as he receives the ball. A better move would be to run the ball at the LH, as shown in *Fig 73*. The IR intentionally runs with the ball at the LH who has to make the decision, in a 2 v 1

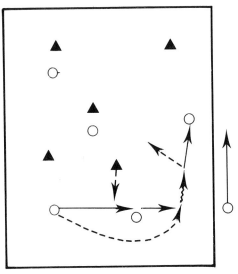

Fig 71

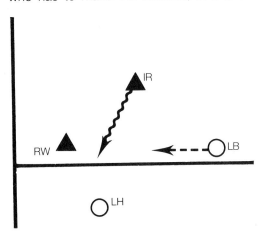

Fig 73

Beating an Opponent
(Figs 72 & 73)

While beating an opponent may be considered an individual skill, its application goes beyond this, and the decision of how to beat an opponent, whether on your own or using other players, becomes a game skill. Often passes are made when defenders have not been drawn out of position and play is made difficult for the receiver.

situation, whether to go for the ball or continue to mark the RW. The IR has to decide if he has drawn the LH enough to pass to the RW who has moved wide or if he should use his individual skill to go between the opposition LB and LH. A player can be beaten by either a pass or individual skill; players must be able to make this choice for the best result for their team.

Losing a Close Marker

This is a combination of movement off the ball and receiving, but is dealt with separately because its application occurs in specific areas of the field, particularly where forwards are being marked man-to-man.

The movement of the player away from the defender should give the player time to receive the ball. The first movement, therefore, is away from the point at which the ball is going to be controlled. The second, returning and changing pace to receive the pass. The two most important aspects are a change of direction to get the opponent off balance followed by an immediate change of pace to get far enough away from the opponent to receive the ball unchallenged. Certainly the change to the obstruction rule has made receiving the ball easier as the obstruction is not a factor to be concerned with.

Passes from the Right

The receiver moves away from the passer to his left, past the right shoulder of the defender. As soon as the receiver is satisfied the defender is moving to cover him the receiver changes direction, accelerating as he does so, back towards the passer, keeping his right shoulder to the passer. This will give a yard and a half of space between the marker and receiver – enough to control the pass with the reverse stick. Having received the ball the player must decide whether he lays the ball off to the passer coming up in support or takes the opponent on himself.

Passes from the Left

The situation is reversed. The receiver will move back towards the passer with his left shoulder to the passer to receive the ball on the open stick. The point of control will be relevant to his next move.

The receiver can now use the new rules to shield the ball from the opponent. However this often causes a breakdown in the flow of the movement. Coaches have to be aware of the value of the new approach to obstruction at the same time realising that constantly receiving the ball facing your own goal and playing the ball back to supporting players gives opponents time to cover and counter attacks that may have been more free flowing.

Vision *(Fig 74)*

Players with good vision are those who can see what is happening in the game and assess situations well – they have an ability to 'read the game'. They see situations within the game developing, anticipate what is going to happen and react accordingly, often before dangers or opportunities arise rather than after the event. It has been said that players either have vision or they have not. I do not believe this; practices and coaching situations can be devised to help players understand game situations and thus improve their vision.

Vision is something that applies to players when they have the ball (individual vision) and when they are off the ball (team vision). Individual vision is related to skill and has been discussed. Team vision is improved when players develop a mutual understanding. Lack of team vision is often observed in club and school hockey where a pass is made and nobody reacts until after the player has made his pass. This results in very few options being available to the player passing the ball. As a player is about to receive a ball those players around him must have started to move prior to his getting the ball, anticipating what passes he is likely to make. Such reactions create more passing opportunities and, therefore, a greater chance of success.

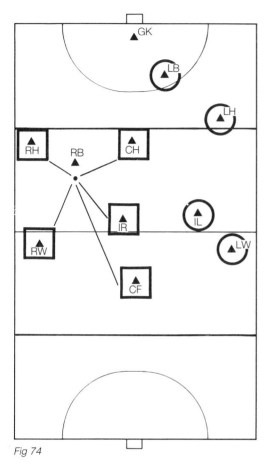

Fig 74

where they can receive a pass away from an opponent. In this instance players are *indirectly* involved but still very much part of the team effort.

To achieve effective results players must be constantly assessing the position of their own players and the opponents in relation to the ball – this is good game vision. Players, who at one instant of the game are indirectly involved with play, must be prepared to become directly involved as the ball moves from one player to another.

Winning the Ball
(Figs 75 & 76)

Many coaches' and players' immediate reaction to the concept of winning the ball is to think of tackling, but tackling is only one part of it. Good anticipation can result in the interception of passes. Both methods of winning the ball are extremely important and must be well practised.

When tackling an opponent, selecting the method of tackling is critical. Timing the tackle, or the interception, is also vital. The art of tackling and its application have been described in Chapter 1.

Interception of the ball succeeds because players are well positioned and have good game vision. They anticipate what is going to happen and time their movement to ensure effective interception. In certain circumstances players have to decide whether it is more effective to mark a player or to go for an interception. Good marking often leads to the opportunity to win the ball by an interception. To go solely for interceptions can be dangerous, often leading to the player's opponent being left free and open for passes. This latter situation results from a player ball-watching and not marking effectively. *Figs 75* and *76* demonstrate these points.

A method of getting this concept over to players is to talk about *direct* and *indirect* involvement. *Fig 74* explains in more detail. The RB in possession of the ball can pass to the RH, CH, IR, CF or the RW. The actual passes will not necessarily be in the direction indicated, but these players must have all made themselves ready for passes and movement off the ball accordingly, they are all *directly* involved with the RB.

The LB, LH, IL and LW should be anticipating what pass may be made to a player with whom they would then become directly involved. They should be moving to a position

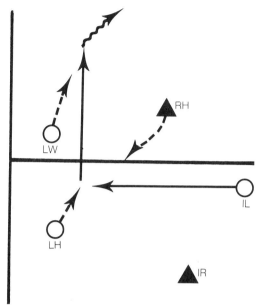

Fig 75

Fig 76

The RH in *Fig 75* has watched the IL and the ball but has lost sight of the LW, the player he is responsible for and should be marking. The ball is passed to the LH, moving up in support, who controls the ball and immediately plays a through pass to the LW, leaving the RH stranded and the LW in an excellent attacking position. The RH could have easily intercepted the pass from the LH to the LW if he had been marking his opponent.

In *Fig 76* however, the RH is in a good marking position, between his opponent and the goal, where he can see both the ball and the opponent. The pass directed to the LW is poor and can be intercepted by the RH who can then move into a good attacking position, linking up with the IR.

Positioning is clearly a critical element of marking, as well as the ability to win the ball by interception or tackling. Players have to quickly assess their opponents' speed and style of play to know when the interception can be made safely. Reckless attempts to intercept the ball can lead to other defenders being put under unnecessary pressure.

Marking and Cover
(Figs 77 to 79)

There are three basic forms of marking to be considered:

1. Zonal marking.
2. Man-to-man marking.
3. A combination of the above.

Coaches have experimented with the first two methods over a number of years and have come to the conclusion that the combination of zonal marking and man-to-man marking in the areas of greatest danger is the most efficient method. The basic pattern is that on losing possession those involved in immediate defence (backs, halves and inside forwards) get on the goal side of the ball; those in the immediate area of the ball – the area of greatest danger – restrict the space available to their opponents by marking tightly. The other members of the team give cover to the area of greatest danger, at the same time being able to move in to close down the area available to their opponent should the ball be switched to another area. This method of defending has the effect of providing cover both in depth and width, and often forcing the opponents to play the ball square having restricted their opportunity to penetrate.

First it is important to look at the basic rules of marking, which are:

1. To be between the opponent and your goal.
2. To be in a position where you can see your opponent and the ball.

available, making it difficult for the opposition LW and CF to receive a pass unchallenged with the LB covering the remainder of the defence. The RB has moved in ready to challenge the opposition IL (observing the basic rules of marking). If the ball was switched to the opponent's right, the LH would be able to move in and restrict the space available to the RW.

In *Fig 77*, the LB has moved into the covering position and the IL has taken up his defensive role by moving in to cover an area of potential danger where he can mark the opponent's movement and restrict an immediate pass to the opponent's RW.

To be able to see the opponent and the ball, the defender has to maintain the position described in No. 2 and move according to the opponents' movement.

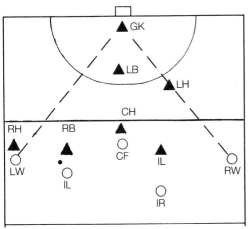

Fig 77   The defensive system shown is 1–2–3–5 but the principles apply to any other formation.

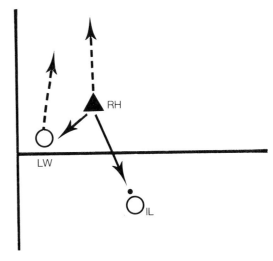

Fig 78

Fig 77 shows the comparison between the position adopted by the RH and the LH. The opposition IL has possession of the ball so the RH and CH have moved in close to the players they are responsible for marking and have restricted the space

In his position the RH can see the player (LW) and the player with the ball (IL) through a reasonably small arc of vision. If the LW moves to go down the line, the RH can adjust his position with ease. However, if the LW moves back to receive a square pass, getting away

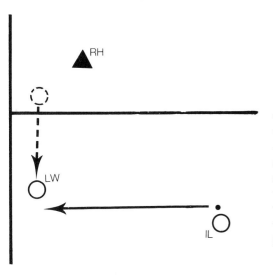

Fig 79

movement of players is required to move that concentration to another area to which play has been diverted.

The area around the opposition LW, who has possession of the ball, is being covered by a series of close triangles: the RH and IR are covered by the RB, the IR and RB are covered by the CH and the RW is closing the area down behind the opposition LW. The IR and IL are covering passes across the pitch, and the LB and LH are giving cover behind the closely protected area. If the ball is moved to the opposition RW, the changes of position to cover the new area of danger are shown. Now in the immediate area the LH and IL are covered by the LB, and the IL and LB are covered by the CH. The RB and RH are covering behind the defence, with the IR and IL covering across the field. The adjustment of players one to another is continuous, as the position of the ball changes, to ensure the cover of the zone is maintained.

Small team games of 3 v 3, 4 v 4 and 5 v 5 can be used to develop the understanding of working within a zone (see pages 38–9). Discipline and the retention of organisation are critical to the success of zonal marking.

from the RH (as shown in *Fig 79*), the RH should not rush forwards to attempt to tackle. He should move into a position to restrict the area for the LW, adopting the attitude 'you may have the ball but you still have to pass me'. The RH is then maintaining the first rule of marking by keeping between the opponent and his goal.

Zonal Marking (Fig 80)

As the name of this method of marking suggests, the defending players form a zone on their goal side of the ball, as soon as possession is lost. Each defender takes responsibility for an opponent coming into their zone of the defence. The zone concentrates on the area of greatest danger, but also ensures cover is provided around the zone should the ball be switched to another area of the field. When this happens, the zone adjusts itself to give concentrated attention to the new area of danger.

Fig 80 shows how, having given concentrated attention to one area, only a small

Man-to-Man Marking

In adopting this method of marking, one defender takes a specific responsibility for one attacker – the RH the opposing LW, the LH the opposing RW, the CB the opposing CF, the RM the opposing IL, the LM the opposing IR. The SW covers behind the defence and the CM in front of the line of the RH, CB and LH, taking responsibility for the opposing CH should he come through in attack.

Man-to-man marking requires an immense amount of discipline from all players. As soon as one player fails to perform his role, or is slow to take up his position, there is an immediate chance that the defence becomes

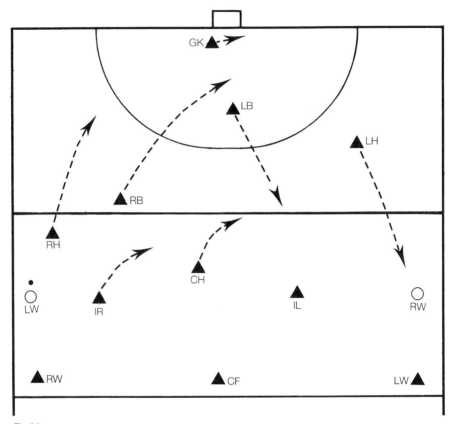

Fig 80

weak and vulnerable.

The only player giving cover behind the defence is the SW, whereas in the zonal method one full back and one half back give cover. I do not believe that attacking play is enhanced by adopting man-to-man marking.

It is worth noting that in the Olympic Games in Barcelona the majority of teams did not use defensive patterns based solely on man-to-man marking.

Combination of Marking Methods

The type of defence best suited to the English style of hockey is a combination of zonal marking first then tight marking of oppo-nents in the area of greatest danger. Adopting this style of defence should provide efficient marking of those players immediately around the ball, providing cover both in depth and width. *Fig 81* describes the movement of players once possession is lost.

The opposition RH has intercepted a pass from the LW to the CF. All eleven defending players have an immediate role to play in forming the zone by marking players and moving to cut off passes or harass opponents with the ball. The LH, IL, LB, CH, RB, RH and IR form the zone. The LW moves to challenge the player with the ball, and CF and RW move to intercept passes that may be played across the field. The LH, IL and

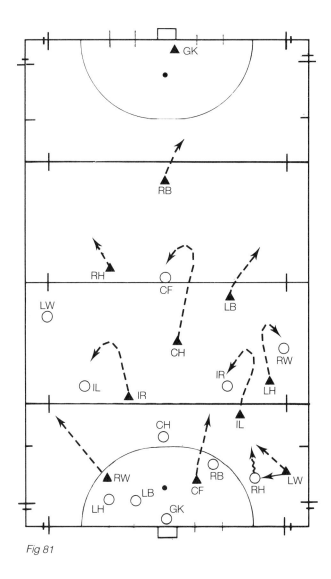

Fig 81

CH have moved to mark the most dangerous players. The IL has relieved pressure on the LB who is able to take up a covering position. If the IL had been further up in attack, the LB would have had to move into a position to counter any attack made by the opposition.

Defence starts at the instant possession of the ball is lost. At this crucial moment the zone must be formed. If any players in the zone are slow to take up their positions, particularly those carrying out a marking role in the area of greatest danger, unnecessary pressure is put on other defending players. Failure to react quickly often results in the opposition gaining numerical superiority in the danger area of the field and thus having a greater chance of penetrating nearer to the defending team's circle.

Counter Attack
(Figs 82 & 83)

When a side has defended deep into its own half the opportunity to counter attack often presents itself. The opposition, having pressed forwards, may leave areas in its own half of the field vulnerable to attack. Counter attacks have to take place immediately possession is lost and at speed, to prevent the opposition having time to get back into good defensive positions. Counter attacks normally take place after a player has intercepted a pass from a position forward in the defence, or from an immediate clearance to a forward. Normally counter attacks are carried out by a single player as a solo attack or by a limited number of players getting forward together quickly.

Having accepted the responsibility to launch a counter attack, the individual or pair of players must be prepared to take on any opponent at speed. Slowing a counter attack down gives opponents a chance to get into good defensive positions and the benefits of the attack are lost. Counter attacks are most effective when players go straight for the opponents' goal in solo efforts, as described above, with support from other players given immediately, or when the point of attack is changed once and the solo attack made immediately the ball is received. This is shown in *Fig 82*.

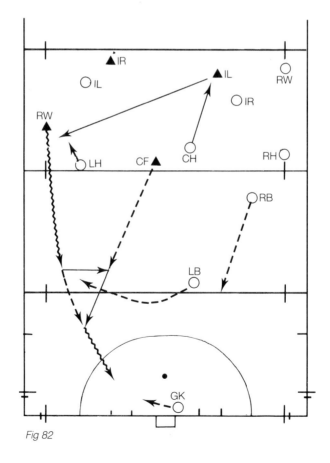

Fig 82

The IL has intercepted a poor pass from the opposition CH. On receiving the ball the IL sees the RW is free and passes to him. The LH is out of position so the RW moves forward with the ball at speed, to exploit the space in the opponents' half. The CF gives support for a wall pass to be played, to beat the covering LB and to enable the RW to attack the circle in a 1 v 1 situation against the goalkeeper.

An ideal small team game to practise counter attack is the 5 v 5 v 5 continuous relay game shown in *Fig 83*.

Having won the ball, the counter attacking players have to get it out of their half of the field in under three seconds, and still retain possession. The O team having lost the ball to the ▲ team go off the field at CD. The Δ team come on to the field. The ▲ team must get the ball out of their own half and retain possession within a limited time, say 3 or 5 seconds. The new opposition Δ team come onto the field to challenge as soon as the counter attack gains possession. Players have to think quickly, the front players moving forwards to be in a receiving position where the counter attack can be started.

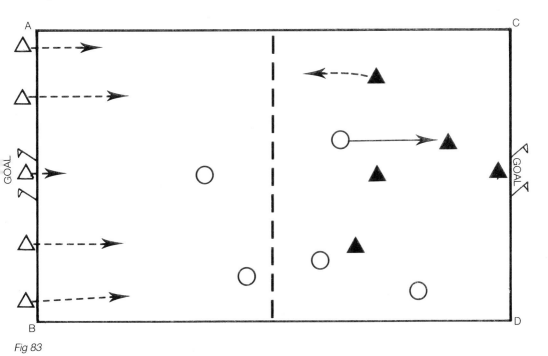

Fig 83

3 Set Pieces

Set pieces occur in the game when the ball goes out of play or the umpire blows for an infringement against a player. There are eight set pieces:

1. Penalty corners.
2. Penalty strokes.
3. Corners.
4. Free hits.
5. Sixteen yard hits.
6. Hit or push ins.
7. The push back.
8. The bully.

PENALTY CORNERS

At a penalty corner, five defenders have to be behind the goal-line and six beyond the half-way line. The attackers may be anywhere on the field of play except the opponents' circle, the only exception being the player putting the ball into play. The intention of the attacking team is to have an effective routine that will result in a goal being scored; the intention of the defending team is to prevent a goal being scored. Both the attacking and defending phases of the corner require planning and practice. Each will be dealt with separately.

Attacking *(Fig 84)*

The attacking players take up positions around the circle, firstly to get a shot at goal and secondly, to be able to pick up rebounds off the goalkeeper's pads or opponents' sticks or to take part in an alternative move to the direct shot at goal. Players H, I and K

are involved with the initial move. Player H controls the ball, so that it is motionless, outside the circle. The ball is then moved into the circle for player I to take a direct shot at goal or to initiate alternative moves. Player K is responsible for injecting the ball from the 10 yard line accurately to the point where it is to be controlled by player H or other players. The players involved in the initial move then follow in to pick up rebounds. Players F, G, J and K are responsible for moving in to pick up rebounds. Player E covers H and I in case they miss the ball. Letters are used for identification here, because players' roles at penalty corners do not necessarily reflect their normal playing positions. Attacking teams will have worked out a set routine and a number of alternatives.

The attacking team may take the penalty corner from either side of the goal. If it is taken from the right, the player stopping the ball may choose to control it and take a shot at goal himself, or to play an alternative pass to a colleague in support.

The essential elements of this phase of attack at a penalty corner are:

1. An accurate fast hit, or push in, to where the ball is to be stopped. The player taking the hit or push in must have one foot outside the field of play.

2. The ball to be stopped immediately. Any delay or misjudgement in stopping the ball increases the defenders' chances of dispossessing the attacking team or blocking the shot.

3. The ball must be stopped dead outside

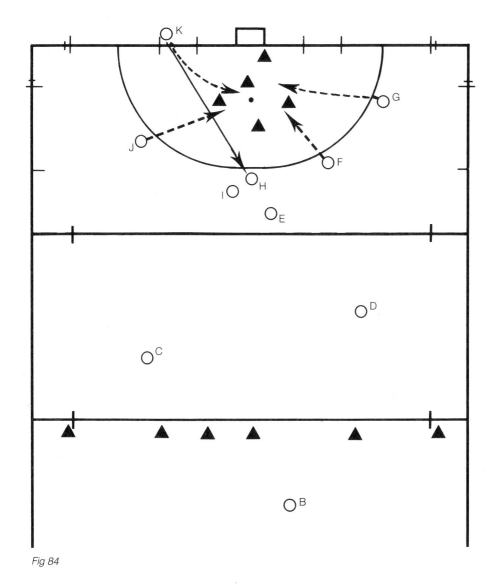

Fig 84

the circle. If the ball travels more than five yards out of the circle it may be played as part of normal play and does not have to be stopped dead. However, to let the ball travel this far from the circle often detracts from the value of the Penalty Corner.

4. The time between the ball being stopped and the shot at goal being made must be as short as possible.

As the shot is made at goal, the goalkeeper will have moved out to narrow the angle of the shot, and the other defenders will start to move out to defend the goal, protect the goalkeeper and attempt to clear the ball from the circle. The remaining attackers around the circle have to move in to collect rebounds off the goalkeeper's pads or the defenders' sticks. Players F, G, J and K move in to form an arc in front of the goalkeeper, far enough away from him to see the rebound, yet near enough to be able to get to it first and attempt a shot at goal. The shooter (I) will follow up the shot for any rebound coming straight back.

Attackers must move in to collect rebounds off the goalkeeper who may go down to block the shot or attempt to kick the ball away. By moving in to challenge extra pressure is put on the keeper, which may cause him to make errors.

Defending

Any good defence to a penalty corner has to be well organised; players must be disciplined and carry out the role, or roles, assigned to them. Basically, there are two phases to a penalty corner defence:

1. The defence for a direct shot at goal.
2. The adaptation of the first phase defence if the attackers switch the ball to a second or more players before taking the shot at goal.

Phase 1 (Fig 85)

The purpose of the defence is to block the shot, to defend against any shot that beats the goalkeeper, and to defend and clear any ball that rebounds off the goalkeeper or other defenders. As in the attacking part of the corner, there are specialist jobs for the defence. The initial line-up is five defenders behind their goal-line, and six beyond the half-way line. The division of these players is not necessarily forwards and defence. The five players behind the goal-line move as in *Fig 85*.

The goalkeeper moves out to narrow the angle, from where he will either go down presenting a 'wall' to the shot, or he will remain standing in preparation to save/ clear any shot. Normally one player – E in diagram – will remain on the line. The goal-keeper will decide with the coach if it is better to position player E to the right side or the left side of the goal. The determining factor in how far the goalkeeper goes out is

that when the shot at goal is taken, he must be still and balanced, ready to take the shot or go down.

Player D is the player assigned to move out to block the opponent's shot, or to hurry the shooter into making a mistake. In getting out to the ball he must be certain not to cross the line of the goalkeeper's (C) vision. He must block the shot with his stick in the open position held by either his left or right hand in a low position, presenting as much of the stick as possible to block the ball.

Player E is responsible for covering the left-hand goal-post and the area behind the goalkeeper, and for any shot that is blocked by the goalkeeper and falls into the segment of the circle behind the goalkeeper.

Players A and F move out to cover the segments in front of and to the sides of the goalkeeper. They also have to be aware of the attackers moving in from the edge of the circle. Player A is given the job to clear the ball off the goalkeeper's pads. They must, in clearing the ball, ensure they do not obstruct the incoming attackers.

The defenders moving back from the half-way line, must hurry to assist the defence. As the ball is played out by the attacking team, all eleven players must move into their positions as quickly as possible. Players H, J and B attempt to get back as far as the twenty-five yard line or the circle to assist the five defenders back to clear the ball out of the danger area of the circle. Players G, I and K position themselves to receive passes as the team moves into attack.

Phase 2 (Fig 86)

If the ball is switched to a supporting player to shoot at goal then the defence has to move from its original position to cover the new challenge. This must not be seen in practice as two separate movements. Defending play-

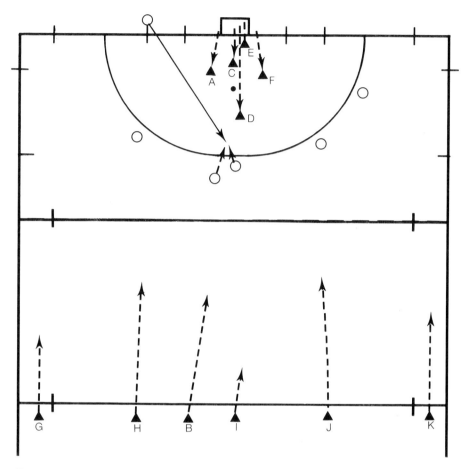

Fig 85

ers, as they move out, will recognise the change by the attacking team. The adjustment in the defence positions is shown in *Fig 86*. Similar readjustments occur for other alternatives the attack may select.

Player A has continued forward from his initially defensive position to put pressure on the new shooter (ensuring he does not block the goalkeeper's view) which probably means blocking the shot with the stick held low in the reverse position and be aware of the free player behind him who will have moved into play after taking the penalty corner. The goalkeeper has moved to his right and is now able to cover the centre of the goal and the right-hand post. Players F and E also adjust their positions to the right. Player D attempts to get back and give additional cover to the centre of the circle. If player D can get well back then player F need not come over as far as in the diagram, thus giving additional cover to the far side of the circle.

At all times, defenders must be adjusting their positions to the movement of the ball and the opponents.

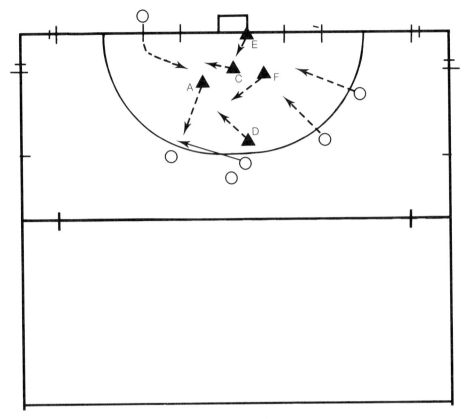

Fig 86

PENALTY STROKE
(Fig 87)

Like the penalty corner, the penalty stroke is a specialist job and must be taken by the person best able to do it, irrespective of his playing position on the field.

The attacker is allowed to take one stride in propelling the ball and may use a flick, scoop or push. The flick is considered to be the strongest, most effective stroke to use. The attacker must, therefore, prepare his position carefully to ensure that when the umpire signals for the stroke to be taken it will be as effective as possible. The problems for the attacker are not so much the stroke but the psychological pressures of taking the stroke. To help overcome these pressures, the fol-

lowing points must be remembered:

1. The player taking penalty strokes should be told of this before the game starts, and a second player should also be prepared in case the first nominee cannot, for any reason, take the stroke.
2. The player taking the penalty should know where he is going to place the stroke before moving up to the ball. If the goalkeeper's position excludes the first choice stroke, then an alternative should have been selected.
3. If the goalkeeper, for any reason, delays the stroke being taken, move away from the ball and relax. Do not remain tensed in the position ready to take the stroke.
4. Remember the stroke is not taken until the umpire blows the whistle.

The approach outlined above results in a positive attitude; indecision by the penalty taker often leads to a weak stroke, giving the goalkeeper a better chance of saving the shot. The point selected by the taker will vary from one player to another. However, near to the corners of the goal is the area most difficult for the goalkeeper to reach, and the top left and bottom right-hand corners are where most strokes are scored.

The goalkeeper should position himself in the goal where he has the best opportunity to move immediately the stroke is taken. The rules insist that the goalkeeper stand on the line; the goalkeeper should, therefore, stand with his heels on the line, in a well-balanced and prepared position.

The goalkeeper will attempt to save the shot with the stick to the right side of his body, or with the leg and body. To the left of his body the shot will be saved by the left hand or body. Above the shoulder on the right of the body presents the goalkeeper with a problem. To play the ball the goalkeeper, therefore, has to decide either to bring the left hand across to save the shot or to hold the stick in two hands releasing and raising the right hand above the shoulder to save the ball. The goalkeeper must look at the position of the taker of the stroke and attempt to anticipate in which direction the ball is going to be played. As soon as the stick goes to the ball the goalkeeper will make his move.

Fig 87   The penalty stroke – note position of attacker and well-balanced position of the goalkeeper.

CORNERS

Attacking *(Figs 88 & 89)*

Corners are taken by the attacking team at a point five yards from the corner of the field on the goal-line, as indicated by the umpire. The attacking team will have planned a number of alternative moves.

In *Fig 88*, if pass 1 is not available, then alternatives 2 or 3, along with others, must be looked for. *Fig 89* shows how the RH can move forward while the RW moves round behind him. As the RH moves towards the circle and defenders come towards him, he will have the option of moving into the circle himself, or passing to the RW who can shoot.

These represent only some of the corner alternatives that can be taken from the right or left. The selection will depend on how the defenders position themselves and which attackers are available. Like the alternatives

described in attacking penalty corners, these moves have to be practised to be effective in match play.

Defending

Defenders again must be organised and disciplined whichever method of defending is selected. Each player within the defence must carry out the role required of him to ensure the effectiveness of that defence. Again, as in the penalty corner, players will have to vary their positions as the position of the ball and opponents changes.

Man-to-Man Defence *(Fig 90)*

The hit being taken from the right means that the attacking CF, IR and RH are immediately the most dangerous players. The CF is marked by the CH and the IR by the IL, freeing the LB to cover in the circle. The LW comes back to take the RH. The LH covers the hit five

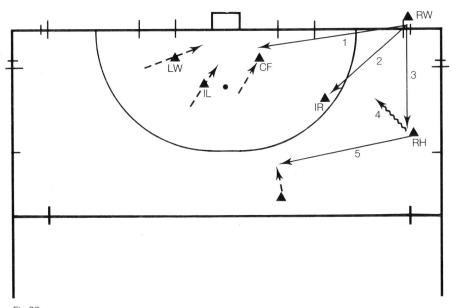

Fig 88

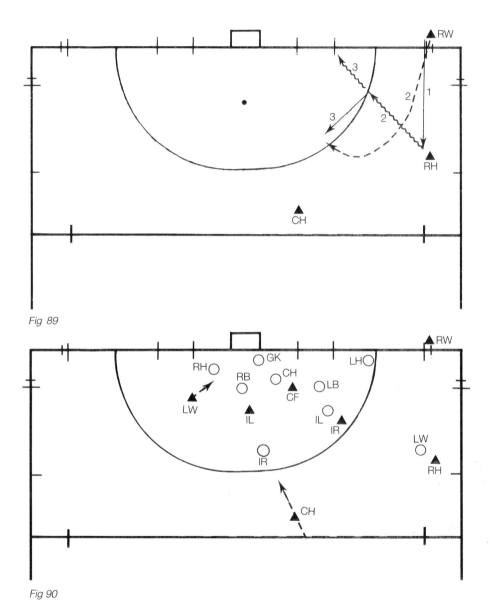

Fig 89

Fig 90

yards away from the RW on the line. The RH, RB and IR are responsible for the attacking LW, IL and CH respectively. In the diagram, they are each in positions where they can move into play as danger occurs, but at the same time they can cover the area of more immediate danger. They can still be said to be marking man-to-man.

Zonal Marking

When adopting a pattern of zonal marking, the defenders attempt to cover the area of greatest danger in the circle. The zone moves and concentrates its attention on the point where the danger arises, at the same time ensuring there is depth and cover in defence.

OTHER SET PIECES

The free hit, sixteen yard hit and the hit or push in have a number of common features to be considered. Each is similar, though taken at different times and from different places on the field. In all cases it is important when taking these set pieces that possession is retained to ensure that an attack can be maintained. Possession will be more likely to be maintained if *space* is well used by those waiting to receive the ball, and by the player taking the hit and if there is *movement off the ball* by those players hoping to receive a pass – this is essential if space is to be well used.

Very often the ball is passed into a crowd of players, making it more difficult for members of their own team to get good control than when a simple pass was available and possession certain. This is shown in *Fig 91* where the RB takes the sixteen yard hit badly (solid line) when an easy pass to the free RH (dotted line) would have resulted in a good attack.

More often than not, passes are available to free players if the player taking the hit has looked around to see who is available.

Fig 92 shows a push in being taken. RH has spotted his CF running into space to receive a pass away from the crowd of players.

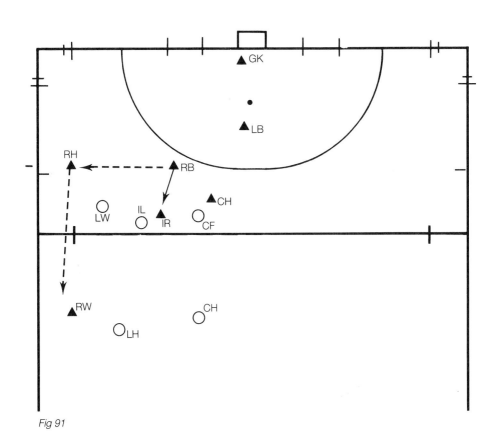

Fig 91

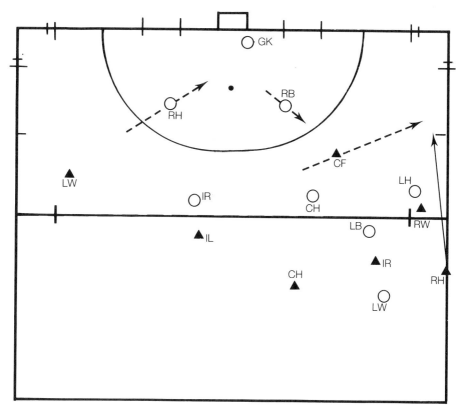

Fig 92

Free Hits

1. The defending team must be five yards away from the ball when the hit is taken.

2. The attacking team can be anywhere, except when the ball is within five yards of the circle when all players must be five yards away from the ball.

3. A free hit awarded to a team in its own defending circle may be taken from anywhere in the circle, or from a point up to sixteen yards from the base line on the line of the offence.

4. A free hit awarded to a team within sixteen yards of its own goal-line may be taken up to sixteen yards from the goal-line, in line with the point where the infringement occurred.

Sixteen Yard Hits

1. A sixteen yard hit can be taken anywhere along a line where the ball went out of play, up to sixteen yards from the goal line.

2. The team not taking the hit, or push, must be five yards from the ball.

3. The ball must be hit or pushed along the ground.

Hit or Push Ins

The hit or push in is taken when a team passes the ball out of play over the side-line. The opposition takes the hit or push in. The team not taking the hit, or push in, must be five yards from the ball when it is played. To gain greatest advantage from this set piece, it should be taken quickly if players

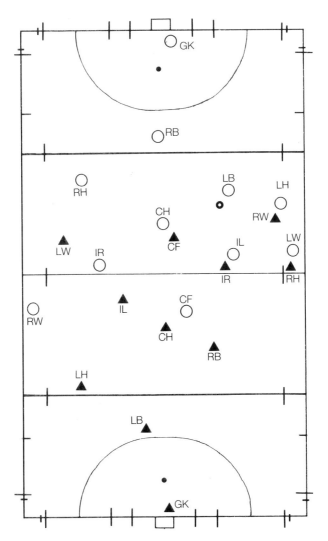

Fig 93

are immediately available. If this is not the case, then space must be created by the movement of players to enable the taker to play the ball away from the congested area. In this instance the hit is best employed.

When defending free hits, sixteen yard hits and hit or push ins, defences must decide whether to adopt a man-to-man or zonal pattern, or a combination of the two, as shown in *Fig 93*.

The attacking LB is taking the free hit. The LH, CH, IL and LW are marked man-to-man, while the other defenders have taken responsibility for other zones of the pitch. The defending CH is close to the CF as danger could occur in that area. The IL is covering any pass across the field, but can move in to the IR if danger occurs in that area of the field. Again, as in other cases discussed above, the defender's position will change as the position of the ball and the opposition varies.

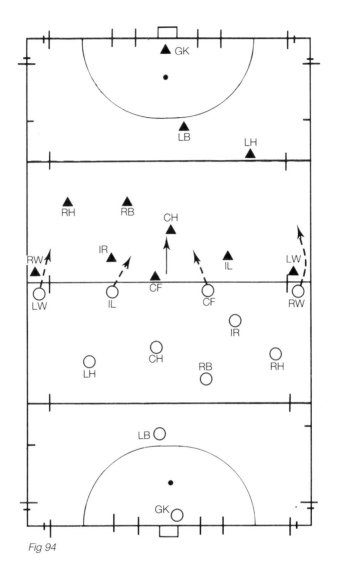

Fig 94

The Play Back

The push or hit back is the method used to start the game, to restart the game after half-time and to start the game after a goal is scored. All the players must be on-side and five yards away from the ball. As the ball is played back the opponents may pass into the other team's half of the field as shown in *Fig 94*.

To ensure that the team in possession at the play back retains the ball, it is best to play it back to the CH, or a player in a similar position, to ensure that the opponents cannot easily get to the ball. The CH then has the option to play the ball either to the right or left before he comes under pressure. Most CHs play to the RH. Coaches will develop their own patterns of play from this point.

The Bully

Although the bully is no longer used to start or restart the game, it is used in the following instances:

1. When the ball gets caught in the goal-keeper's equipment. The bully is taken either on the spot where the incident occurred or five yards from the goal-line, if the incident occurs within five yards of that line.

2. After an injury, if the game is not started with a free hit.

The players taking the bully should stand facing each other with their right shoulders facing their own goals. The bully is performed by touching the ground with the stick then raising it above the ball three times.

4 Team Formations

Team formations are difficult to operate effectively if a player does not have a basic understanding of the general principles of team play. Too often players in the early stages of learning hockey are thrust into an eleven-a-side game before they are capable of coping with its demands. In consequence their progress is slow and often the full potential of a player is never realised.

In some schools where fixtures become more important than coaching a player may, for example, be put on the right wing for his first match, do quite well, and remain there throughout his school playing time. In fact this particular individual, if he had been allowed to develop progressively, may have been a much better left side defender. The development of team play must be through small team games, like mini-hockey, seven-a-side hockey, where players enjoy a greater involvement in the game and have more ball play contact time enabling them to develop the individual and team skills required to play the full eleven-a-side game.

TEAM FORMATIONS AND THE PLAYER

Team formations can be misleading if considered to be a rigid arrangement of players on a field. They are a starting point on which a team bases its particular style of play. Each player within the team must understand thoroughly that he has a role both as an attacker and a defender. When a team has possession of the ball all the team are attacking and when the opponents have possession of the ball all the team are defending. Team formations will be selected to suit the players involved; some show little difference one to another, while others differ considerably. Small changes can be made to the patterns of play if a particular opposition's strength has to be countered. Selection must be positive and based primarily on your own players' strengths, not because a particular player is going to be in the opposition team – that must be a secondary consideration, important as it may be. There is a danger if coaches are over-concerned with countering opposition strengths that the team's attitude may become too defensive and their ability to attack overshadowed. It is my personal belief that teams who are prepared to attack are more likely to be successful: over the years the Australian, German, Dutch and Pakistan teams are excellent examples of this approach, and the most likely to succeed on artificial grass. However, having accepted this attitude it is also important to realise that when possession is lost defence has to be adopted immediately so that the ball can be repossessed and a further attack mounted.

THE 1–2–3–5 FORMATION (Fig 95)

Up until the mid-1960s hockey was played to one basic tactical formation with five forwards, three half-backs, two full-backs and a goalkeeper. It could justifiably be argued that this formation was in fact 1–2–3–2–3 as this is the way it was (and is) played, with the five forwards in a reversed 'W' formation. This

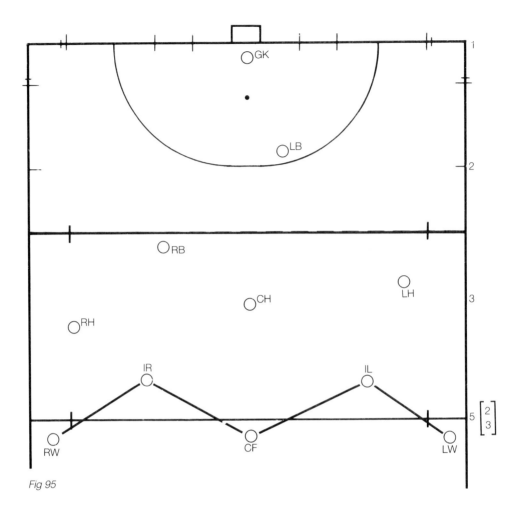

Fig 95

formation is still widely used by schools, clubs and representative teams and has much to commend it. The great strength of this formation is the pyramid, which is formed by the five forwards and the centre-half with the right-half coming into attack, which gives a strong attacking pattern. The passing alternatives available are considerable and attacks can be made using the whole width of the pitch. The triangles formed by groups of players within the formation give not only width but good support in attack, as well as cover in defence.

The weakness of the 1–2–3–5 formation lies in the way the two full-backs are expected to operate. Depending on which side of the field the ball is, one full-back will be marking and one covering.

In *Fig 96* the RB is forward engaging the IL who has the ball, and the LB has taken up a covering position, with the CH marking the CF. The LH takes a part marking position. The defence has to adjust to the change in the point of attack as shown by the movement of the RH who is marking the LW. However, if the ball is switched quickly to the opposition IR, a 2 v I situation (IR and RW v LH) can develop before the LB has time to move into an effective marking position. Moves are made to the opposition by the RH, RB, LB and LH as indicated by the dotted lines. These are big areas for defenders to cover when the ball is moved quickly and accurately, and controlled immediately by the opposing team. Any

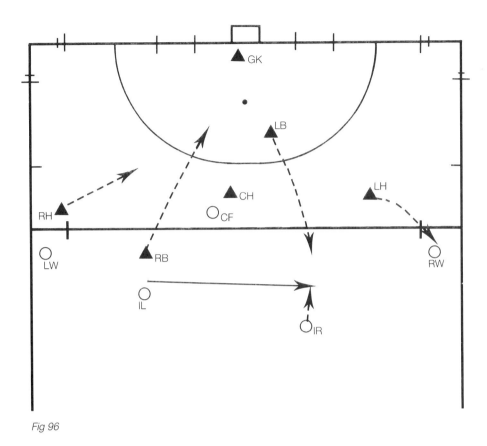

Fig 96

delay by the attackers gives the defence time to readjust their positions, but against a quick attack this defensive formation can have problems. Therefore other players in the team have to assist with defence, in other words the whole team must defend. The inside forwards particularly have an important part to play in alleviating the problems of the defence by covering back and accepting a defensive role when the opponents have the ball.

The defending IL in *Fig 97* must move back to get on the goal side of the opposition IR. This now removes the problem for the LH who, if the ball is switched to the right, can give his full attention to marking the RW, the player he is responsible for, and the LB can move forward to a covering position behind the IL which gives greater defensive strength in depth.

Defensive play in the 1–2–3–5 formation is based on zonal covering and marking the opposing players tightly in the area of the ball (the area of greatest danger), the remaining players positioning themselves where they can cover that area and move in to mark the players they are responsible for when the ball is switched.

The importance of discipline and organisation in defence has been stressed as a basic principle. *Fig 98* represents a typical attack. The ball is played by the attacking RW and intercepted by the opposition LH. At that point

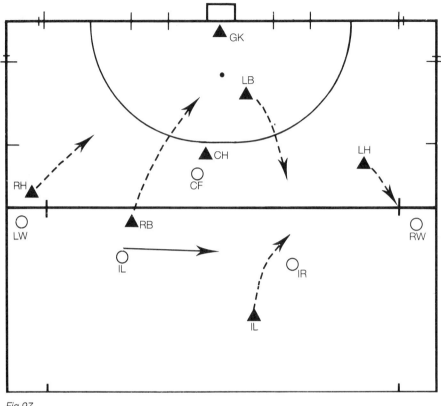

Fig 97

possession is lost and the team must defend. The dotted lines indicate the immediate action that should be taken by the now defending team. The RH, IR, RB, CH, IL, LH and LB have all moved to form a defensive zone from which they can face the oncoming attack. The RW has moved in to challenge the LH who has the ball. From this position of strength the defending team can adjust their positions quickly, effectively and in an organised way to any attack made by the opposition.

As a team moves in to attack when possession is gained, the whole team must move as a unit, giving depth to the attack. Players should keep in touch with each other to provide a number of passing alternatives. As the attack is mounted the basic pattern of 1–2–3–5 may change. Remember this is the basic pattern from which the team works, not a fixed pattern.

The example of a team in attack in *Fig 99* shows how a team changes its formation according to where the ball is. The team has mounted its attack through the RW with the other four forwards taking up positions to attack the goal. If this attack breaks down there are a number of players available to cut out passes from the opposition, and at the

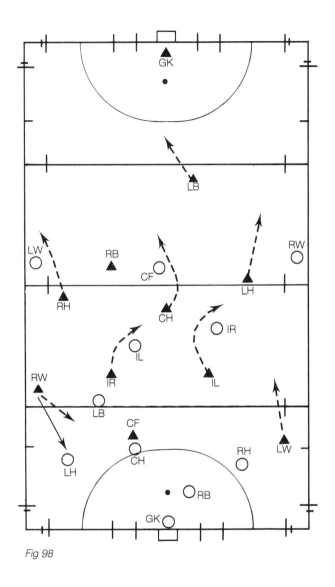

Fig 98

same time the RW has good support enabling him to make telling passes. The left of the field does not need to be defended at this stage but, if necessary, it can be covered quickly by the LH and LB. The dotted lines indicate the lines of approaches made by the RH, CF, IL and LW as play is built up in reaction to the RW move to attack the opposition goal-line.

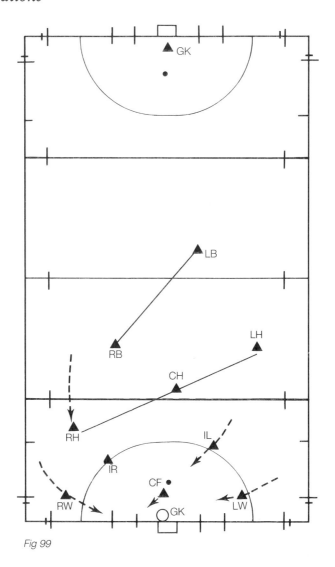

Fig 99

OTHER FORMATIONS

Since the 1960s, rule changes, defensive thinking by coaches, greater fitness of players, initially a need by European countries to find tactical methods of overcoming the Asians' greater skill levels, and an increase in the number of tournaments, encouraged coaches to experiment with a variety of tactical formations. In doing so players have been given different roles from those in the 1–2–3–5 formation, often with different position titles. However, it must be remembered that whatever formation a team selects there are two phases of the game – attack and defence – each requiring a change of role and mental attitude by the players concerned. It is often misleading to give too much attention to diagrammatic descriptions of playing positions as the game is constantly moving. However, the following are examples of alternative playing formations.

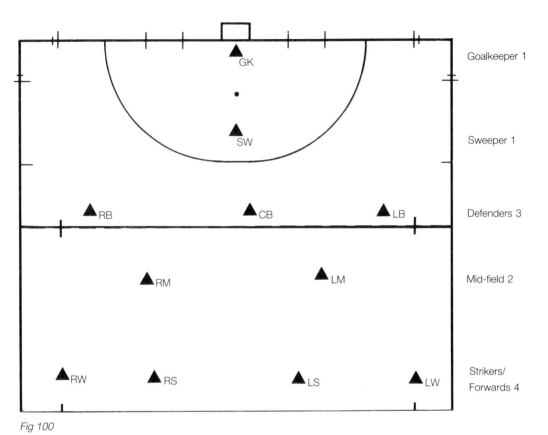

Fig 100

The 1–1–3–2–4 Formation *(Fig 100)*

In this formation the sweeper takes the role of the covering full-back, taking up a non-marking position, covering the players involved in front of him and intercepting passes which penetrate the line of three defenders. The centre-back marks the opposing centre-forward or central striker, the RB the opposing left-winger, and the LB the opposing right-winger. The two mid-field players, RM and LM, mark the opposing inside forwards; should the opposition centre-half come through, either the RS or LS would have to drop back and assist their own defence. This is assuming that the opposition is playing 1–2–3–5. Should they be playing another pattern, the coach would have to decide how he is going to deploy his players to cope with the changing situation. It should again be emphasised that there is a weakness in being too rigid in playing patterns; coaches and players have to realise that the team in possession of the ball dictates the defence that should be adopted.

In the 1–1–3–2–4 formation the workload required by the right and left mid-field players is considerable. They require assistance from the backs to give width in mid-field when attacking, and from the strikers to come back and feed the ball forward, as they gain possession and move into attack. The danger of this pattern of play is that it becomes too defensive and not enough players get up into attacking positions.

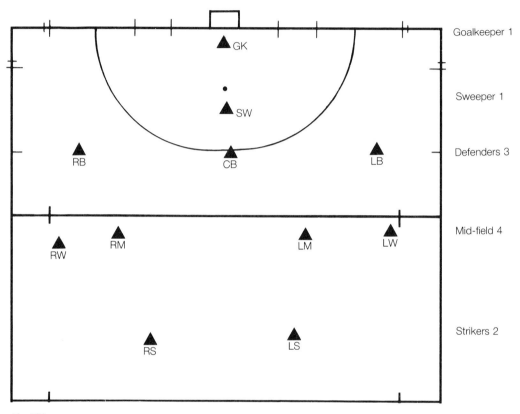

Fig 101

	Goalkeeper 1
	Sweeper 1
	Defenders 3
	Mid-field 4
	Strikers 2

The 1–1–3–4–2 Formation *(Fig 101)*

The basic pattern of this formation is similar to that of the 1–1–3–2–4 except that the RW and LW are moved back to strengthen the mid-field and to spread the workload in that area. As possession is gained, the wingers move forwards to assist the strikers. Often width is gained in mid-field but lost in attack. It also takes longer to mount effective attacks as the ball has to be held by the two front strikers while they wait for support to come forward. Used against a team that is known to be stronger than your own, this pattern can assist in reducing the opposition's scoring power, but at the same time it can limit attacking effectiveness.

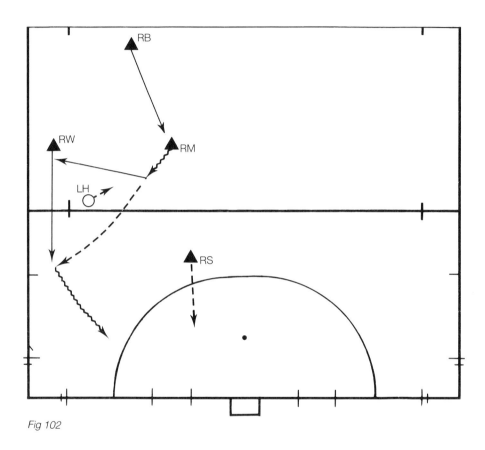

Fig 102

Having gained possession, the attacking triangle on each side of the pitch – RW, RM and RS, and LW, LM and LS – have to develop an understanding that will create flexible movement. An example is given in *Fig 102*.

The RM, having received a pass from the RB, passes square to the RW and then moves diagonally to receive a through pass from the RW. The RM now takes the RW position and must maintain that position to attack the opposition's goal-line. The RW would then move further in-field to cover the area vacated by the RM. This type of flexibility can upset opposing defenders.

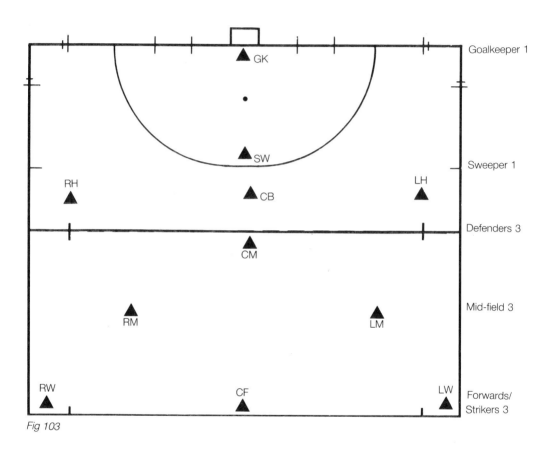

Fig 103

The 1–1–3–3–3
Formation *(Fig 103)*

This particular formation is the one most used by Dutch and German international teams in recent years. The operation of the formation is applied differently by various coaches, particularly the roles given to the three mid-field players. If they are given primarily defensive roles the result will be a lack of players in attack when possession is gained. Basically, there are three patterns formed by the mid-field players – the straight line, the triangle and the inverted triangle.

The Straight Line

The line formed by the RM, CM and LM is not necessarily horizontal, it will tilt as players move to cover dangerous, or potentially dangerous, moves by the opposition.

The Triangle (Fig 104)

The three mid-field players form a triangle (with the CM positioned behind the two others) that is almost identical to the triangle formed by the CH, IR and IL in the 1–2–3–5 formation. The fundamental difference is their marking roles. The RM and LM in this formation will mark the opposing inside forwards or mid-field players.

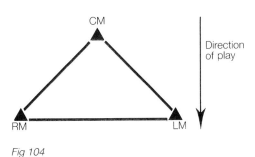

Fig 104

The Inverted Triangle (Figs 105 & 106)

In this arrangement of players, the CM plays in front of the RM and LM and behind the three forwards, acting as a support forward. This arrangement of players has the advantage of allowing the RM in particular to attack from deeper lying positions, often playing off the CM and moving into the opposing circle decisively at speed. Balls played to the CM from right or left can quickly be changed to the opposite side of the field by the CM thus changing the point of attack.

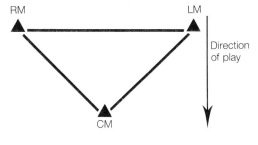

Fig 105

With the CM playing forward of the RM and LM, he has to adjust his position carefully with the CF. There is a basic rule to be observed. The two should imagine themselves related to the points of a square, and never being on the same line. Positioning this way improves the chances of the ball being received by the CM and then played into space for the CF, and the opportunity to receive the ball away from a marking player. If the CM and the CF are either one behind the other or side by side on the imaginary square, the passing opportunities are often reduced.

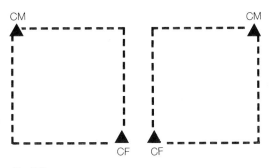

Fig 106

CHOOSING THE FORMATION

A philosophy for team tactics is formed from one of two basic attitudes. Team tactics are either based on (a) attack first and defend strongly when possession is lost or (b) defend from a strong base and attack when you can. Within either of these approaches, because hockey is an ever moving and changing set of circumstances, nothing can be black and white. However, the coach's basic belief will greatly affect his approach to team tactics.

Coaches who adopt the attack first philosophy are prepared to take the game to the opponents, attempting to get more players into an area of attack than there are opponents. Of course, when play breaks down and possession is lost defence is crucial and an organised and disciplined counter to the opponents' attack has to be established. The length of time between your side losing possession and taking organised action to defend is crucial – this time gap must be the absolute minimum. It is at this point that games are won and lost.

Conversely, if coaches adopt a basic defensive attitude and start by getting as many people into defence as possible, working from a very solid base, the crucial point for them is the change from defence to attack and getting enough players for-

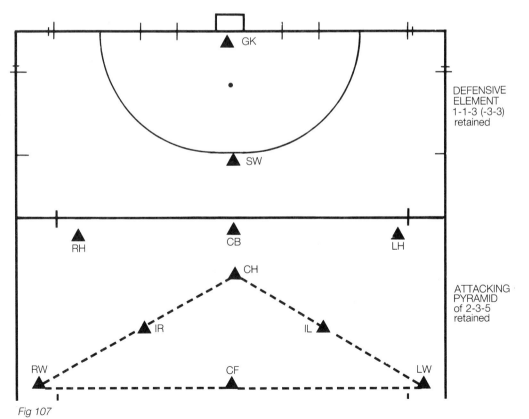

DEFENSIVE ELEMENT
1-1-3 (-3-3)
retained

ATTACKING PYRAMID
of 2-3-5
retained

Fig 107

ward to enable their side to score goals. Sides that base their play on defence often have to be strong counter-attacking sides to win matches.

My personal choice of playing formation, assuming the necessary players are available, is a combination of formations using the strengths of the 1–2–3–5 in attack and the strength of the 1–3–3–3 in defence. To use this combination formation requires players who are fit and able to adapt from habits formed over previous years. The basic approach is to *attack* and then *defend*. Attack the opposition, take the game to them and defend immediately possession is lost. Too many coaches in this country have allowed their attitude to be *defend* and then *attack*. The positions players are nominated within the formation is important, particularly for those who play in the middle of the field. It has become apparent over a period of years that those players who are given the role of midfield players RM, CM and LM adopt a primarily defensive attitude. Therefore I nominate them IR, CH and IL which seems to result in the players adopting a more attacking attitude, providing that very important 'pyramid' formation in attack shown in Fig 107. The RH moves up to extra width to the right side of the attack in the middle area of the field.

In defence (i.e. as soon as possession is lost) the initial movement is to zone and then mark zonally players that come into the area of the field for which the defender is responsible. The pattern of defence adopted will vary according to the formation being adopted by the attack.

During the 1983 Champions' Trophy in Karachi, it was interesting to see the Indian team experimenting with a formation different to the 1–2–3–5 that they have used almost exclusively over the years. They brought their centre forward back into mid-field, from where he played the role of an attacking CH, and moved their CH to a more defensive position. This pattern created an arc of four players at the back which moved according to the side of the field from which play came. The formation gave a solid defence, but when possession was gained the Indians had great difficulty in getting enough players up into attack.

Through all the descriptions of tactical patterns, it can be seen that the coach must look at the strengths of his players before deciding to adopt a particular formation. Before making changes, the coach must be certain that changes would result in improvement over what is already being played. Changes require practice and preparation; they cannot be employed without these.

Artificial grass pitches have seen many international teams, like Britain's 1988 Olympic Gold winning squad, come full-circle by adopting the 1–2–3–5 system. But whatever the chosen formation, the principles of team play remain the same.

5 Captaincy

THE CAPTAIN AND CAPTAINCY

In any team, be it a school, club or representative eleven, the captain holds an extremely responsible and important position. He must lead by example, more than any other person, both on and off the field. The extent of any captain's responsibility in a team will depend on how many individuals form the team management group. At school, this is usually the member of staff in charge of the team, plus the captain. In a representative team, there will probably be a team manager, team coach and captain. In a club team, more often than not, it is the captain on his own, though more and more clubs are using coaches with their senior and junior teams. At this stage the representative team area will not be considered, the remarks will be confined to the captaincy of school and club teams.

Regrettably, too many club captains are asked to do the job with no coach to assist them, the captain having to adopt the role of team organiser, coach and captain – far too extensive a task for anyone, other than the really outstanding individual, to do well.

The remarks made about captaincy here have to be considered in conjunction with the role of the coach. The captain has to work closely with the coach; once a team takes to the field of play the captain takes control. If changes to plans have to be made, the captain must be able to take such action. For example, if the team's attacking penalty corner routine is not working, the captain may instruct the number two striker to take over.

Who that person is will have been decided by the coach before the game has started. Where a team does not have a coach, the captain will have greater responsibilities which can be divided into three phases:

1. Before the game.
2. During the game.
3. After the game.

Where a team does have a coach, 1 and 3 will be his responsibility. In some cases, where a team secretary is involved, certain of the responsibilities in 1 and 3 will be his tasks. The division of these responsibilities, therefore, depends on the people available. In this chapter they will all be outlined.

Before the Game

There are a number of responsibilities:

1. To ensure that training programmes are well organised, with meaningful and interesting tasks for players, based on the weaknesses shown in the last match and the requirements of the next match (coach/captain).
2. To ensure those playing in the next game have good notice (coach/captain/team secretary).
3. To ensure arrangements for each game are all in order (captain/team secretary).
4. To ensure your team meet in good time for each game. Home games, one hour before the game; away games, in time to arrive at your destination one hour before the game (coach/captain).
5. To ensure all members of your team are

Fig 108   In this international between Germany and Australia, close control
         by the German player has enabled him to avoid the tackle.

fully aware of the patterns of play, and set piece roles are clear to all those in the team (coach/captain).

6. To greet the umpires and visiting team, and ensure they have adequate changing facilities (captain).

7. To ensure your team has a good warm-up (captain/coach).

During the Game

The captain has to take responsibility for maintaining the pattern of play and directions issued by the coach prior to the game. Where aspects of play are not operating successfully, he will make adjustments as he sees fit.

The captain's main role on the pitch is to encourage and help the members of the team. The example set by the captain is extremely important. Each individual member of the team is different, they have to be treated differently when things are not going well for them. When things are going well the captain's job is easy; if things go badly for the team or an individual, however, the captain must respond and try to overcome the problem, at the same time not letting his own game suffer. How the captain deals with any problem will differ from occasion to occasion. If the team is not doing well, the captain must try to lift their performance by encouraging and reminding them of the important points which will improve their play as a team.

When the problem is with an individual the captain must, again, encourage and if criticism is to be made, it must be constructive. Some players react to a sharp reminder of points by the captain, while others require much gentler treatment. The captain must learn how to deal with each individual to get the best from particular players. If an individual continues to play below his best the captain, where a coach is not in attendance, will have to consider making a substitution.

At half-time the captain, when a coach is not present, must cover those points necessary to ensure the team continues to play as they have been, if the game is going well, and finish the game successfully with a win. When things are not going well, the captain must pick out one or two points to help those players who have been experiencing difficulties to overcome them. The remarks made must motivate and lift players to ensure that they are ready to get back into the game to lift their performance.

At half-time the captain must keep his remarks short, sharp and to the point. It is better to say too little than too much. Whatever is said, the final points should be to encourage the team as a whole. Destructive criticism must be avoided at all times, it is better to say nothing to an individual than make a remark that is going to destroy a person's confidence.

After the Game

Immediately the game is completed, the captain should:

1. Thank the opposition captain for the game.

2. Thank both umpires for controlling the game.

3. Ensure that those players in the team who have played well are complimented, and that any player who is displeased with his performance is encouraged and helped.

4. Ensure that the opposition and umpires have adequate showering facilities and that after changing, tea or refreshments are available.

5. At tea, ensure that your team mixes with the opponents and umpires. Remember to be gracious in defeat, and humble in victory.

6. After the game and tea, make a note of those points that need to be covered in the next training session and game.

The captain, where he is not working with a coach, must listen to advice and comments made by club spectators and members of the team, sift that information in his mind and then make his own decisions.

SELECTING A CAPTAIN

It is easy to decide that the best player should be appointed captain of a team. This may not be the best choice – a captain needs to be more than a good player. The factors to consider in selecting a captain are:

1. Is he a player who is respected by the team?
2. Has he good leadership qualities?
3. Is he a responsible person, and prepared to accept responsibility?

4. Is he a good enough player to justify his position in the team?
5. Is he, on being appointed captain, going to find that the responsibility has a disruptive effect on his game?
6. The person selected as captain must be able to discuss team matters with the coach and feel able to make constructive criticism.
7. Liaising with other team captains in the club. The captains of the teams below the club 1st XI should advise the captains of teams above them on players who they feel should gain promotion to a higher team. Successful club team captains often feel a reluctance to let a good player go up a team. Captains must consider the progress of individuals, allowing them to play better hockey.
8. The selected captain must have a sense of humour.

6   Coaching

THE COACH AND COACHING

Here, the coach as an individual and the task in which that individual is involved will be discussed.

The coach must have the fullest possible knowledge of the game to operate at the level at which he is working. The style used to impart that knowledge will vary from person to person: some quiet and persuasive, some aggressive and ruthless; both, as has been proved, can be successful. The role of the coach, as it is applied to hockey is twofold:

1. To assist individual players to realise their full potential.
2. To blend the individuals into a harmonious and successful team.

The first task is like that of the violin teacher, the second the conductor of the orchestra. The team will be as good as the individuals in it, the coach having to blend their strengths and create a successful playing unit. To achieve these aims the coach must have a thorough knowledge of what each individual requires in terms of technique and the appreciation of that technique in the game. It is useless a player being able to perfect the technique of pushing if they cannot use it effectively in a game. Practices designed and used by coaches must ensure that skills are used in game-like situations. The knowledge that a successful coach requires can be placed under the following general headings.

Individual Performances

1. The technique of the game. The hit, push, tackling etc. and how to demonstrate the techniques.
2. How the techniques can be transferred to skill practice situations which are relevant to the game of hockey.
3. The ability to recognise faults as they occur.
4. Rectifying faults and thus improving the individual's performance.
5. How to motivate players to improve their own performance.

Group Play

This applies either in open play or set pieces.

1. How to work separate individual performances into group play.
2. How to create an understanding between individuals within a group to gain the optimum performance from the group.
3. How to rectify faults in group play, isolate them and rebuild them back into improved group play.

Team Performance

1. Understanding the various methods of organising teams in terms of playing formations.
2. Recognising weaknesses and strengths in opposing teams' tactical play.
3. Exploiting opponents' weaknesses and nullifying their strengths, by adjusting your own team's pattern of play.

4. Recognising a breakdown in your own team's tactical play.

5. Rectifying those faults by rebuilding the specific aspect of play back into an improved team performance.

6. Thoroughly understanding the use of substitution.

The total knowledge a coach requires is considerable; much is gained only by experience and has to be stored for occasions when it is needed. Selecting the correct information to cope with a specific situation is one of the main arts of coaching. The amount of knowledge used at any one time should be the minimum needed to allow the individual to progress. This is a factor often overlooked by coaches; too many give too much information at any one time which can confuse players.

There may be occasions when a good demonstration has been given and some youngsters require little further help. This gives the coach time to spend on those needing more help. The importance of a good demonstration by a coach cannot be over-emphasised. Demonstrations fall into two clear categories:

1. Those that show how skills are carried out by good players, often given to motivate.
2. Those given to show the young player the basic movement from which he will develop his performance.

The coach who has been a good player should remember that he has possibly developed an individual style which he should take into account when giving a demonstration of a basic movement.

ORGANISATION

Lack of organisation and preparation often leads to uncoordinated, poor quality coaching sessions. The coach must know what he wants to achieve in a session; this can only be done with good planning. At the same time, however, he should allow for flexibility within the programme to cope with any unforeseen problems. Variety in a programme maintains interest. Use different practices from session to session, and within sessions for the same technique; a variety of learning situations which will widen a player's experience.

The planning and type of practices used will vary according to the level of ability and the numbers taking part. Availability of equipment may also affect what can be done. The essential point is that the practice must be relevant to the game of hockey. Where possible it must progress from simple to more complex playing situations, moving logically from one practice to the next and into the game.

The types of activity used should also be carefully considered. Often a small team game or a grid practice gives a far better learning opportunity than the eleven-a-side game. Practices can be divided into groups as follows:

1. Continuous relays.
2. Grid practices.
3. Group practices.
4. Small-sided games.

The coach has to ensure that there is a link, however small, between the practice and the game. Static practices must be avoided wherever possible. An example might be where one player passes to another who controls the ball and passes it back, and so on. What relevance does this have to the game of hockey? How many times in a game do players pass the ball back and forth to each other in this way? There is almost no relevance to the game at all. Consider, however, a simple passing practice done in a grid.

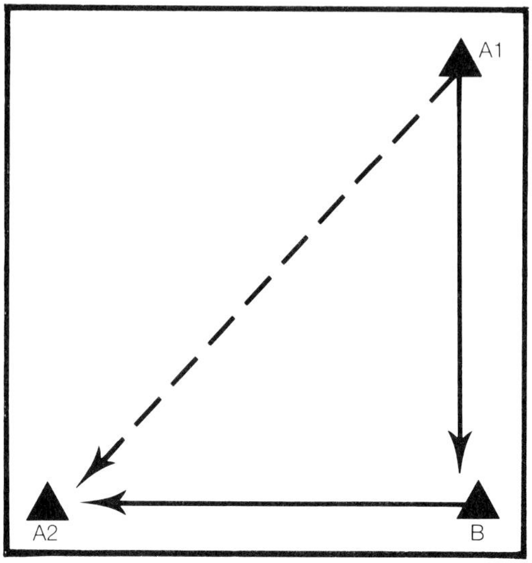

Fig 109

In *Fig 109*, A at position A1 passes the ball to B and moves to A2 diagonally across the square. B controls the first pass and plays it to A2 for A to control. The practice is then repeated in the reverse order with A moving from A2 to A1. Consider the game content in this practice in comparison to the static example:

1. The pass by A to B is *a square pass.*
2. The movement of A from A1 to A2 is *movement off the ball.*
3. The pass from B to A2 is *a through pass.*

These three elements looked at collectively give us the triangle as a basic unit for hockey. The grid gives the players guide lines for the square and through pass which are performed in a reasonably confined area. All these movements though simple are extremely relevant to the game.

Continuous Relays

Continuous relays give an excellent opportunity for individual skills to be practised in either a competitive or non-competitive way. As well as giving the opportunity to practise a technique and put it into a skill situation, they encourage the player to perform a movement and move to a new position. The value of this to the game is that, having made a pass or a movement, players have to think about their next move – whether to support, cover or create space for another player to move or pass the ball into. The following example of a continuous relay demonstrates this point.

Fig 110

A runs with the ball towards B and at the half-way point pushes it to B who receives the ball and starts to move towards C to repeat the exercise. Having pushed the ball, A moves to take B's place, and C, on receiving the ball, continues the movement towards A. This sequence can be adapted in a number of ways or used in a triangle.

Grid Practices

Coaches must realise these practices do not have direct relevance to a pitch. Coaches must, therefore, ensure that they move onto the pitch, to give players a greater understanding of space and purpose. Where possible the practice should be opposed and finish with a shot at goal. The example illustrated in

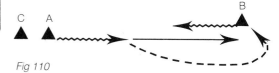

Fig 111 is the simple grid practice into a game situation.

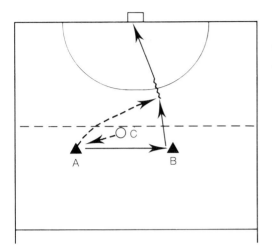

Fig 111

As A is challenged by C the ball is passed square to B who plays a through pass for A to move on to, collect and move into the circle for a shot at goal. To organise this type of practice on a single pitch requires cones or corner flags to make the goals.

Continuous relays and grids cater for a large number of players, particularly beginners, in reasonably small areas. Normal grids are 10 metres square and can be used singularly or in groups, according to the number of players involved in the practice.

The advantage of this method of organisation is that all the players involved can be easily observed as the coach moves round the area, going in to help players as and when necessary. If the coach attempts to conduct the session from inside the grid area he will only be able to see part of the group at any one time. Working from outside, the coach has a complete view of all the activities and, therefore, has a greater chance to observe faults

and any dangerous situations that may develop.

Continuous relays can be operated by using grid lines as starting and finishing lines, or lines on the pitch, i.e. 25 yard line to halfway, or other obstacles for marking off grid and pitch areas. The optimum distance for continuous relays is between 20 and 25 metres. Not all coaches will have the luxury of a grid area but this should not deter them from using grids. Cones, bricks, wooden blocks, flags and other objects can be used to mark areas.

Coaches should also consider where they conduct their practices. More often than not the actual playing field is the least suitable surface to use for skill practices or technique learning. The playground, tennis courts or sports hall are often far more suitable than grass areas, in that they provide a smoother surface which enables the learner to develop good habits. The markings of a netball court, for example, give six good practice grids by dividing the thirds of the netball court down the centre.

Group Practices

The coach must be looking for general and individual faults. If general faults occur then all the group should be called together, the points of weakness explained and how they can be improved demonstrated. How the coach organises a group to give this type of demonstration is important. The group must be in a position to see the coach and those players who are being used for the demonstration. From his position the coach should have a view of the players and the watching group, so he can address both easily. If the coach were on the same side as the watching group he would have his back to them and immediately the possibility of losing their attention arises.

Where the coach wants to work on an

individual or a small group, again positioning is important. The coach must stand far enough away to see all the group and to talk clearly to them as well. Being too close, even with a small group, can result in the instruction becoming too chatty, with loss of attention from some players.

Within a coaching session the coach must ensure a balance of technique learning, skill practice, small games, and the full game. The amount of time given to each section will depend on the standard of the players the session is designed for. Wherever possible coaching sessions should comprise:

1. A thorough warm-up.
2. Skills learning, practice or revision.
3. Game related skill practices in open play situations and set pieces.
4. Small-sided games or the full game.

The Use of Competition

Hockey is a competitive game. It is, therefore, necessary to ensure that coaching work involves some form of competition. The amount of competition must be balanced between the opportunity to learn and improve skills and the chance to test what has been learned. The method of competition used will vary. In the early stages of learning competition must be so that all the players, whether good or bad, have a target which can be achieved and improved. The better players should not be hindered in reaching their potential, but at the same time competition should have meaning for the less able. The initial grid practice already referred to, can be used to illustrate this point.

In *Fig 112*, the eight players are all performing the same practice, two in each square, with A, C, E and G doing the running. The practice

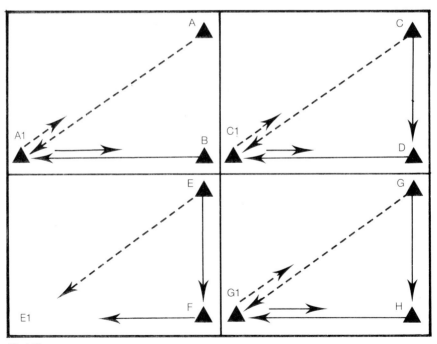

Fig 112

is repeated for one minute; each player running counts one point each time he returns to his original position. At the end of one minute, their scores may vary from five up to eight points. B, D, F and H now do the same exercise for one minute. The competition has to be designed so that each pair has a realistic target to aim for. Two targets are given to the group as a whole, each has to beat his opponent's score but everybody is also attempting to beat eight. This method of competition motivates each pair to achieve a higher score than before. Not to include a target for each pair could destroy one pair's desire to improve as they would have great difficulty in obtaining the highest score.

Continuous relays can also be competitive. Take, for example, a practice involving running with the ball. A runs the ball to B and takes B's position, B runs to C and so on. Here the coach can set two forms of competition, which are equally applicable to grids.

1. The winning group is the group that can get the ball across the area first.
2. A time limit can be set, say two minutes, the winning team being the one which can get the ball across the area in that time.

For younger players the first method of competition is the more suitable. Young players enjoy competition provided it is well structured. It instils a positive approach and purpose to an activity creating the response required in match play.

Progressive Practices

Coaches must structure practices to enable players to move easily from one stage to another, understanding each stage as it develops into a more complicated form. Each stage must have a purpose which the coach fully understands both technically and how it

fits into the structure of the progression in use. The following series of practices is used to show a full progression from a basic practice to a game-like situation on a pitch. If practices are well structured they will produce the performance required from players without a great deal of technical information being given.

Stage 1 (Fig 113)

The simple grid practice already described giving a pass right to left. The first pass is followed by movement off the ball, the second pass is into a space.

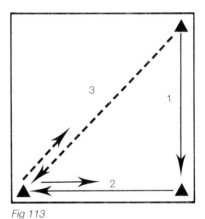

Fig 113

Stage 2 (Fig 114)

The passes in this practice are still right to left but both players are moving diagonally across the square having made their pass. Timing now becomes an important factor to ensure the pass and the player moving off the ball reach the corner of the square at the same time.

Coaching

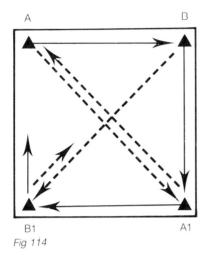

A　　　　　　　　　　B

B1　　　　　　　　　A1

Fig 114

Stages 1 to 3 cater for two players per square who can be doing the same practice. The coach will introduce competition to sharpen performance. Specific coaching should not be done during periods of competition, but between competitive sessions. General coaching points can be used to remind players and sharpen their approach to the competitive element.

Stage 4 (Fig 116)

Four players operate in one grid square; a set sequence of passing is established – 1 to 2, 2 to 3, 3 to 4, 4 to 1. At the same time all the players must keep moving. This ensures that players are having to be constantly aware of the position of the others in the grid, particularly the player to whom they have to pass. The ball must be received in such a way that enables the next pass to be made easily and with the minimum of adjustment.

Stage 3 (Fig 115)

All passes are now left to right creating a more complicated movement of the body to get into the passing position after receiving the ball. As players improve, they will change their method of receiving the ball so that it becomes more relevant to the next passing move they have to make. Being a more difficult movement, the timing factor increases.

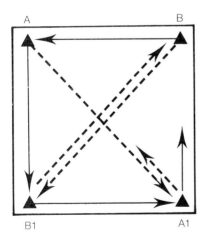

A　　　　　　　　　　B

B1　　　　　　　　　A1

Fig 115

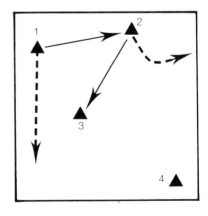

Fig 116

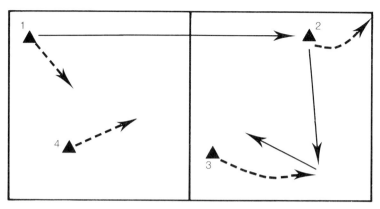

Fig 117

Stage 4a (Fig 117)

The same practice as in Stage 4, but over two squares. The selection of the method of passing to cover the required distance is a new factor. The combination of hit and push passes are used. The area over which the players have to be aware of the movement of the other players is also increased.

Stage 5 (Fig 118)

One of the four players now becomes an opponent creating a 3 v 1 game. The three have to get as many consecutive passes together as they can. The further away from the opponent players keep and the further they are from each other within the grid, the more difficult it is for the opponent to gain possession. Added factors now become apparent – movement off the ball can either take an opponent away or make a pass possible. The most effective pattern of passing to retain possession is that experienced in Stage 1.

All the practices up to Stage 5 have lacked a directional sense. However the plus factors outweigh this weakness. Directional play can be added from Stage 6 onwards.

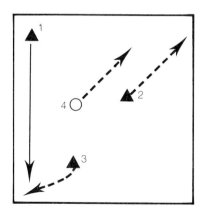

Fig 118

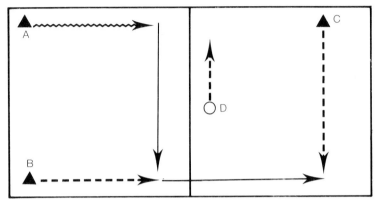

Fig 119

Stage 6 (Fig 119)

A and B either move with the ball or pass it towards the midway line of the two grids. D, the opponent, may only move along the half-way line. A moves with the ball towards the half-way line, drawing D out of the centre to intercept. Having done this A passes square to B, out of D's reach. B immediately controls the ball and passes it through to C who has moved off the ball to collect the through pass. New coaching points have now been added:

1. Moving with the ball to draw a player out of position.

2. An effective square pass while running with the ball.
3. Positioning to receive a square pass behind the line of the ball.
4. Receiving the ball in a way that enables a quick through pass to be made into space before the opponent can recover.
5. Movement off the ball to collect a through pass.

All these skills are essential in the game and are practised repeatedly within a confined area.

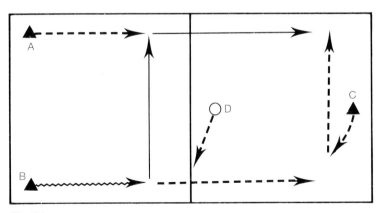

Fig 120

Stage 6a (Fig 120)

The practice starts as in Stage 6 but B moves with the ball to draw D out of the centre of the double grid. D must move in this way to cut out a straight pass by B to C. Having drawn out D, B makes a square pass to A who receives the ball, controls it, and immediately makes a through pass to C. B, seeing the through pass being made, moves into C's square so that B and C can operate the practice in the opposite direction attempting to play the ball past D to A. The practice now becomes continuous, with the player not passing moving into the opposite square to support the receiver of the ball.

Stages 1 to 6a have all been performed in grid squares. It is important to progress the practice onto the pitch, so that its game relevance can be seen by the players in terms of positions. They will experience different problems receiving in the left wing position to those in the right wing position; these must be understood and practised.

Stage 7 (Fig 121)

Three groups of four players, A, B, C, D; E, F, G, H and I, J, K, L, work in different parts of the field. The movements performed are as Stage 6, with the addition that the receiver of the through pass, having controlled the ball, con-

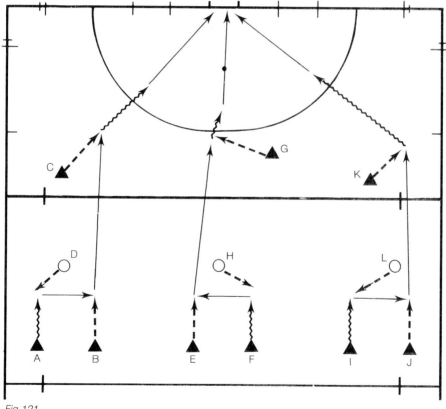

Fig 121

tinues to the circle and makes a shot at goal. The coach must organise the sessions so that groups attack the goal in turn. Having made the shot at goal, players must move wide of the other groups coming in, as they return to their positions.

Stage 7a

Once the coach is satisfied that the basic movements in Stage 7 have been completed satisfactorily, he can add three further elements to the practice (as described below), bringing the activity near the game situation by introducing competition.

1. The players starting with the ball (A, F, and I) can either pass the ball to the supporting player or make a direct through pass themselves. This adds a small element of decision-making for these players, and also increases the problem for the defenders.
2. As soon as the through pass is made, the defenders (D, H and L) can attempt to get back and prevent the strikers (C, G and K) getting a shot at goal. This puts considerable pressure on the strikers.
3. The player not making the through pass now moves up to support the striker, as in Stage 6a, giving the striker an alternative pass if the defender gets back in a position to defend a shot at goal.

The speed with which the coach moves from one stage to the next will depend on the speed with which the players master the previous stages. Where there is a breakdown at one stage it may be necessary to go back a stage to perfect the skills being used.

Stage 8 (Fig 122)

An extra defender is now introduced into each group. This defender, P, is brought into practice to mark the striker.

E and F repeat the initial move. G moves in anticipation of a through pass from E, taking P out of the centre of the field. E passes the ball square to F and, as it is received, G accelerates away from P to receive the through pass from F. F's pass must be into space away from G to give him the opportunity to get away from P. G then attempts a shot at goal or passes square to E for him to shoot.

Stage 9

Play attack and defence, attempting to use these moves as and when possible. If the opportunity arises and the move is not used, the coach should stop play and point out where the move could have been made.

Stage 10

The full game, ensuring players use the moves as relevant in the playing situation. For some players remember the full game might be mini or seven-a-side hockey.

It will not be necessary to go through all the stages of any particular progression at any one time. What stages are used will depend on the level of the players the coach is working with. It will, however, be necessary to work from the simpler moves to the more difficult: for some from Stage 1 to Stage 6, for others Stage 6a to Stage 7 and so on. The coach must assess the development he requires and adapt the practices to what he wishes to achieve.

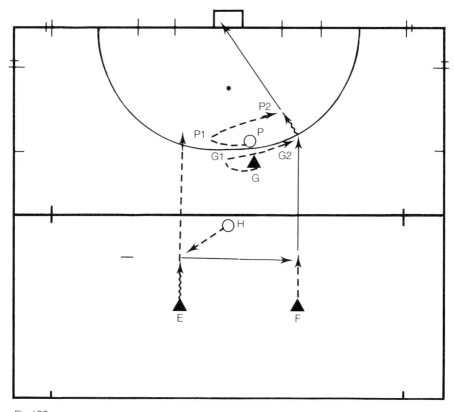

Fig 122

COACHING IN THE GAME

Coaching in the game, be it in small team games or the full game, is more difficult than coaching techniques and skills in practices; progress is often slower. Coaches must not become irritated or frustrated if they do not achieve their required target immediately. It has to be remembered that there are far more factors involved in a game situation. The transiency of a game provides an increased number of stimuli which the player has to assess before making decisions and taking new ac-

tions. In skills practices and technique learning, set movements are often performed, so it is far easier to recognise reasons for success or failure.

In the game situation the coach should work to themes, for example developing attack on the right side, moving the ball quickly out of defence, or support and width in attack. The movements required by the team in possession of the ball must not be too stereotyped; if they are, the defenders will be able to counter them. Variations may have to be used, with players having to take decisions of their own according to the problems they face. The coach has two tasks – to recognise the reasons for breakdown, and to correct the fault causing the breakdown. While this is similar to the process adopted in techniques coaching, correcting faults is not such a precise task.

The coach must develop a sense of anticipation for what is likely to happen, and when a fault occurs recognise the breakdown. The game should be frozen, if necessary moving players back into positions at the point of breakdown, and the coach must go through the movement, explaining what errors were made and how they can be corrected. The coach should point out to the players where they were, what they did wrong and how they could improve the movement by altering their position in relation to other players and the man with the ball. Coaching in the game requires quick thinking on the coach's part and immediate positive action when a fault is seen. Too long a delay often makes it impossible to re-create the situation of the fault.

The coach should question players, asking why they reacted as they did in a particular situation, and what could they have done to improve that move. Players often see their errors and understand their mistakes better when questioned.

The coach has to decide whether the error was a skill fault, or a fault of a player off the ball who had, perhaps, positioned himself badly. To establish full knowledge of any breakdown the coach must see the movement within the game. Bringing the game back to the point of error enables the player to identify his mistake and to understand how it can be overcome. The coach has either to show the individual how a change in skill could have improved an aspect of play or how other players, by their positioning or response to particular stimuli, could have reacted differently and improved the aspect of play being corrected. For example *(Fig 123),* an error might occur when LW passes the ball back to IL, who controls the ball facing LW, thus making himself unaware of what is happening on the right-hand side of the field. The coach has to show the player at fault that if he had allowed the ball to pass across his body before controlling it, his vision of the right-hand side of the field would have been improved and the number of options available to him increased.

The coach can only solve problems in this way if he has been able to see the complete picture. At the point when IL receives the ball, he freezes the game and is able to point out the complete picture to the players, explaining the game situation and how the play can develop tactically. To gain this ability coaches must have made a study of tactical play by watching good matches live and on video recordings. English hockey teachers and coaches often do not watch enough good hockey to enable them to develop their ideas.

When freezing a game, solutions to problems can often be solved by questioning players involved in a tactical movement. Having re-created the point of breakdown the coach should ask players what they could have done to avoid the breakdown, to make them aware of their options in play.

Where coaches find that faults in tactical play are recurring it may be worthwhile conditioning the game. This means imposing certain temporary rules on play to achieve a particular end. For example, if your team are failing to play any successful square passes and play the ball forwards too often unsuccessfully, the condition could be that every alternate pass must be square. This is 'overcorrection' but it has a twofold benefit. Firstly, it makes the player with the ball think over a wider angle of distribution and secondly, it makes the players off the ball conscious of making themselves available for the square pass.

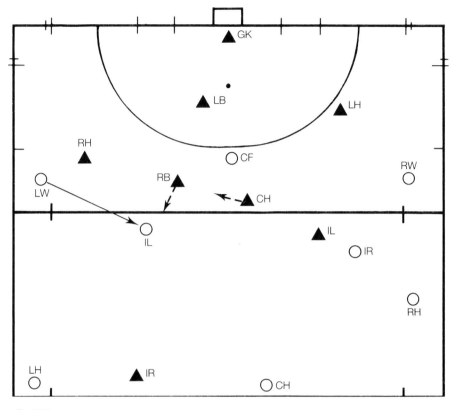

Fig 123

The conditions the coach imposes temporarily will vary. Coaches will find that experience tells them which condition gets the best result. Below are some conditions that I have used when particular problems arise.

Problem Too many diagonal passes are being intercepted by opponents.
Condition When attacking, a square pass must be followed by a straight pass, if necessary into a space.
Problem Players are too often running with the ball.
Condition On receiving the ball only three touches of the ball are allowed – one to control, two to adjust, three to pass. It is interesting to note that this condition often results in the game opening up and more space being created.

Problem Players are playing too close together.
Condition Every third pass must be hit more than 20 metres.
Problem Players pass when their own team members are being marked.
Condition To run with the ball at opponents to create a 2 v 1 situation.
Problem Players are not getting back in defensive positions quickly enough (often 'ball watching').
Condition As soon as possession is lost, players must get back on the goal-side of the players they are responsible for marking.

Where coaches can get an umpire for coaching in game sessions, he can be asked to emphasise certain aspects of play, for example where young players are developing dangerous habits like swinging the stick when hitting, the umpire can be asked to over-emphasise the danger element in an attempt to cut out wild swinging of the stick. The umpire may also be asked to be lenient on certain aspects of play to allow the practice game to flow and tactical moves to develop.

FURTHERING COACHING KNOWLEDGE

The art of coaching, like many other activities, has become far more sophisticated in recent years. It has become more than teaching a player to hit or push the ball, or how to centre during a game. Advances are being made by sports science and medicine, enabling the coach who wishes to further his knowledge to have a far wider understanding of the art of coaching. This new knowledge enables the coach to understand the reason behind a movement, to understand individuals more thoroughly and to see that problems can be approached in different ways. The benefits are considerable for those who wish to improve themselves as coaches.

Contributions come from sports science (physiology, biomechanics, etc.) and sports medicine (treatment of injuries, psychological problems, and how to deal with them). In addition, aspects of coaching have been aided by the use of man management, visual material and other methods of communication. The information being presented by these agencies will assist the coach to do a better job. The coach, however, has to decide what knowledge he requires and how he is going to use that knowledge in his coaching work. It is important to realise that there are subjects relevant to coaching hockey beyond the pure hockey content of the coach's work. The higher the level of work, the greater the degree of familiarity with subjects outside the pure hockey content will be required.

7 Fitness and Training

Modern day hockey requires that players who wish to take the game seriously realise the importance of fitness. In the past there has been too much play in relation to preparation. Preparation includes improving skills, tactical understanding and fitness. Fitness must be looked at as more than running and a few exercises; fitness training has to be seen as an ongoing planned part of a player's preparation.

Training is broken down into two parts: pre-season and during the season. The pre-season element of training is extremely important as it sets the stamina-strength base from which specific fitness for the game can be added. During the season, training has to be planned to maintain fitness levels, and to raise these levels for particular events, or important games.

Most clubs do not have the facilities that enable them to train effectively during the winter months, so players often have to train on their own. This chapter deals with the general principles of training; more detailed information on training can be found in a number of publications, particularly the Hockey Association coaching handouts and the National Coaching Foundation's booklet *The Body in Action*.

Hockey is an activity that requires a player to last seventy minutes of walking, jogging, running and sprinting for varying distances and speeds – very different to the athlete who may be training to sprint a 100 metre race once a week. Hockey requires individuals to have a good endurance capacity (aerobic endurance) and strength to enable a player to delay the point at which fatigue sets in. Once fatigue starts to affect a player there is a greater chance of a lowering of skill performance and decision-making.

A hockey player has to ensure that he understands some of the aspects that assist effective performance. These are: endurance, strength, speed, flexibility and skill. The latter has been discussed in previous chapters.

Endurance and Strength

These should be concentrated on in the pre-season period. Endurance work requires long-distance running which will improve the ability of the heart's capacity to get oxygen around the body. Players should run over measured distances and time each run. In addition to endurance work, players should be improving their strength levels through weight training. This can either be done with free-weights or by using multi-gym equipment. Whichever method of weight training is used, players must seek advice on how to use equipment properly and what exercises to do.

Circuit training can be used both with and without equipment. The style of circuit training used will depend on the facilities available. Circuits can be designed for players to do this area of training on their own, in their own homes. Circuits must be well structured and timed; as times improve, the load (number of repetitions of exercises) is increased. The sequence of exercises within a circuit must be balanced – legs, abdominal, arms, etc., rather than one leg exercise followed by another leg exercise.

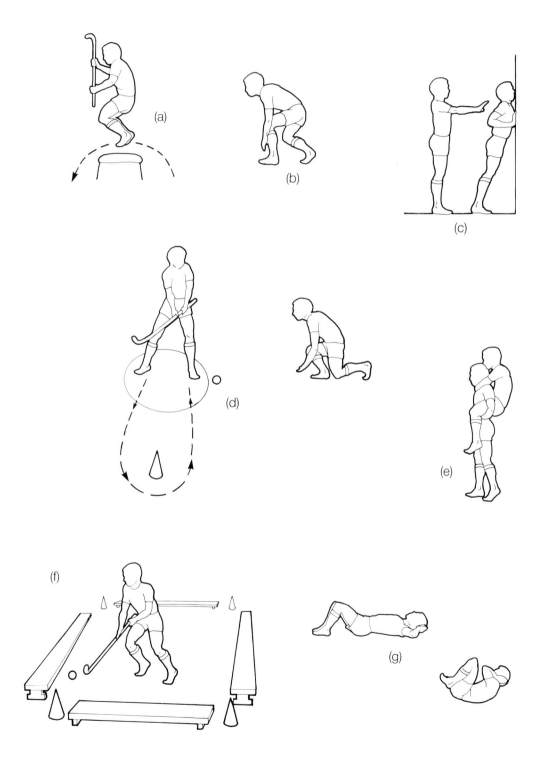

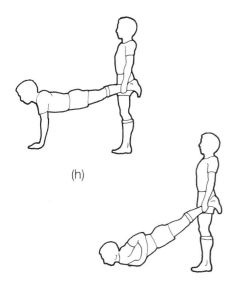

(h)

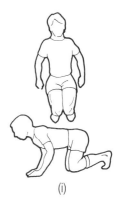

(i)

Fig 124   Hockey circuit – (a) box jump;
(b) ankle running; (c) wall press;
(d) control and pass; (e) partner carry;
(f) dribbling maze; (g) knee and chest
raise; (h) elevated push-up; (i) depth
jump.

Speed

Once the levels of endurance and strength have been improved, players are able to work on speed with greater effect. The type of speed required varies according to the demands of the player's position. Different positions require varying distances of speed work. Coaches must ensure that wherever possible, training schedules are designed for each player. Speed in hockey can be looked at as a number of components:

1. Speed without the ball.
2. Speed with the ball.
3. Speed on the turn to recover.
4. Speed of reaction.

All these elements must be covered in a training schedule.

Flexibility

Flexibility is an important part of overall fitness. Good flexibility and a good range of movement will assist speed and endurance performances, and more importantly reduce the possibility of muscle strains and tears. A regular pattern of exercises should be done each day. A good range of flexibility is a major factor in the prevention of injury.

Warm-up

Warm-up before training and matches is essential. The body must be prepared for vigorous activity, which is likely to occur at the very start of a game. Stretching must be a part of the warm-up; this is particularly important for goalkeepers. Too few hockey players in clubs warm up thoroughly, consequently they take part of the game to warm up and therefore do not, during that period, produce their maximum performance. In addition, they are more likely to pull or strain muscles.

8 Equipment

Every year hockey equipment becomes more sophisticated. Manufacturers are always looking for improvements in the shape of the head of the stick, the weight of goalkeeping equipment and other changes, to attract buyers to their goods. Goalkeeping equipment, while becoming lighter, provides virtually complete protection. The range of stick sizes has been extended to cater for players from age eight to senior club teams. A variety of hockey balls are available, from cheap composition balls or expensive leather balls for grass play to dimple plastic balls for synthetic grass use. The range of equipment is extensive and to the uninformed bewildering. However, for every player, whatever their age or size, there is now suitable equipment. Instead of sawing off the handle of learning sticks for youngsters there are now sticks of suitable size and balance.

Sticks

The range of hockey sticks available on the market is extensive. The rules of the game specify that a stick can weigh up to 28oz with no regulations about length. The stick must pass through a 2in ring. At most major tournaments and competitions, and occasionally at club games, umpires will check that sticks pass through the 2in ring.

The head, for competition, should be made of wood; mulberry is almost exclusively the wood used, though some heads are made of laminated wood. There are experiments being carried out to produce plastic sticks for the educational and recreational market. Most top class players like their sticks to be as stiff as possible, and often also have them stiffened with fibreglass. The cost of sticks varies a great deal; this often depends on how much work has gone into the handle of the stick. The plastic-type sticks that are being produced are ideal for use on playgrounds, tennis courts and other hard surfaces. These sticks are ideal for introducing hockey to young players.

The length of sticks available covers the requirements of anybody wishing to play the game: they range from 28in to 38in. The normal range available is:

28in and below for children 6–7 years old.
30in–34in for children 8–12 years old playing mini-hockey.
34in–38in (normally 36in) for children aged 13+ and adults.

Most adults use a stick of 35–36in weighing around 20oz. Some senior players will use a heavier stick (23–24oz) particularly if they are involved in hitting penalty corners.

Balls

The surface that hockey is played on often determines the type of ball used. Match balls, where the game is played on grass, can be selected according to the limit of funds available. Dimpled plastic balls have been developed for use on artificial grass, with no seam and the effect of the dimpled surface makes them run extremely well over the smooth surface.

Mini-hockey balls are made of plastic and weigh 3½oz. This ball enables young players to pass and control the ball with greater ease. Coaches working with boys and girls up to 12 years of age should consider the mini-ball a must. The ball can be moved over greater distances both when pushing and hitting which results in better use of space and greater understanding of the tactical aspects of the game.

Other hockey balls available range from composition balls, plastic-covered balls, those with simulated leather, and leather balls, some with seams and some without. While the more expensive balls are clearly the best for competition, the middle price range is ideally suited for practice and school games.

All balls whatever their quality should be cleaned for each game and be adequately supplied. A dirty ball is often difficult to see and therefore becomes dangerous.

Boots

When choosing a pair of hockey boots it is important to ensure that they give good support to the foot, some cushioning to the heel and that they are really comfortable. The surface on which you are going to play will determine the studs you use: longish studs for wet, soft ground, and short studs for dry, firm grounds. Synthetic grass requires an 'astro' boot; these now come in a variety of types. It is important to have footwear that is going to provide comfort on the firmer surface, to alleviate strains on muscles and tendons.

Players should try a number of boots before making up their mind, remembering that good quality boots are worth paying the little bit extra for.

Shinguards

No player should play without some form of protection to the shins. These can vary from a simple football-type pad to a guard that cov-

ers the shin and ankle bones. The modern type of boot used for hockey ideally requires players to use pads with the extra ankle protection. Shinguards come in varying sizes and can therefore be purchased to give comfort that will not hinder movement.

Gumshields

Many players now wear gumshields to protect their teeth. Injuries to the mouth do occasionally occur, caused either by a rising ball or stick. It is sensible to encourage all players to wear gumshields to avoid damage to the mouth and teeth.

Goalkeeping Equipment
(Fig 125)

There has been considerable development in the production of goalkeeping equipment over the past few years. There is now no excuse for a goalkeeper not having the complete confidence to do his job well. Many young players have been completely put off playing in goal because of knocks received as a result of inadequate protection from substandard equipment. Goalkeeping equipment can be expensive, but money spent on good equipment is an excellent investment in ensuring any goalkeeper's safety.

Helmets

Goalkeepers must wear a helmet to ensure they have good protection for the face and head. In selecting a helmet the goalkeeper must ensure the helmet fits well and that he has good vision, and that his sight is not hampered in any direction.

Fig 125   Goalkeeping equipment .

Gloves

Goalkeeping gloves are designed to give padding on the outside of the right glove, in which the stick is held, and on the palm of the left glove to avoid bruising when saving shots with the left hand.

Some goalkeepers wear cotton inner gloves to ensure the goalkeeping glove fits snugly. Gloves must fit comfortably and allow the stick to be easily held. Some gloves are the gauntlet type and give extra protection to the wrist, but these can be rather cumbersome.

Body Protection

Goalkeeping equipment to protect the body is now very sophisticated and offers complete body protection. When a goalkeeper goes down to make a save the whole of his body is protected. A complete kit of body protection equipment is expensive but absolutely essential if a goalkeeper is going to be effective. Padded shorts and upper body clothing ensure that any goalkeeper can be confident that any part of his body coming in contact with a shot is protected.

This equipment should be provided by clubs and schools for all their goalkeepers, since very few youngsters can afford to buy their own goalkeeping equipment themselves. No goalkeeper should be expected to keep goal unless he is adequately equipped. Goalkeeping is a dangerous activity and must be responsibly approached by all those asking any player to keep goal. Before purchasing equipment take advice from your coach.

Useful Addresses

The National Governing bodies for Hockey are the Hockey Association – the governing body for men's hockey, and the All England Women's Hockey Association – the governing body for ladies' hockey. The Associations are structured to look after the game at various levels, both having regional and county organisations who look after the clubs and schools in their area.

Further information about the Associations and the services they offer can be obtained from:

The Hockey Association,
Norfolk House,
102 Saxon Gate West,
Milton Keynes MK9 2EP

The All England Women's Hockey Association,
51 High Street,
Shrewsbury SY1 1ST

Both Associations conduct courses for coaches and players. Information about these courses can be obtained from the Directors of Coaching for the associations at the above addresses.

Index

Index

Other Titles in The Skills of the Game Series

American Football	*Les Wilson*
Badminton	*Peter Roper*
Basketball	*Paul Stimpson*
Canoeing	*Neil Shave*
Cricket	*Keith Andrew*
Croquet	*Bill Lamb*
Crown Green Bowls	*Harry Barratt*
Endurance Running	*Norman Brook*
Fencing	*Henry de Silva*
Fitness for Sport	*Rex Hazeldine*
Flat Green Bowls	*Gwyn John*
Golf	*John Stirling*
Gymnastics	*Trevor Low*
Judo	*Tony Reay*
Karate	*Vic Charles*
Netball	*Betty Galsworthy*
Orienteering	*Carol McNeill*
Rhythmic Gymnastics	*Jenny Bott*
Rowing	*Rosie Mayglothling*
Rugby League	*Maurice Bamford*
Rugby Union	*Barrie Corless*
Skiing	*John Shedden*
Soccer	*Tony Book*
Sprinting and Hurdling	*Peter Warden*
Squash	*Ian McKenzie*
Strength Training for Sport	*Rex Hazeldine*
Swimming	*John Verrier*
Table Tennis	*Gordon Steggall*
Tennis	*Charles Applewhaite & Bill Moss*
Trampolining	*Erika & Brian Phelps*
Triathlon	*Steve Trew*
Volleyball	*Keith Nicholls*
Waterskiing	*John West*
Windsurfing	*Ben Oakley*
Women's Lacrosse	*Bobbie Trafford & Kath Howarth*

Further details of titles available or in preparation can be obtained from the publishers.